# AMERICAN ACTRESS

# The Mormon Presence in Canada

# The Mormon Presence
# in Canada

EDITED BY

Brigham Y. Card

Herbert C. Northcott

John E. Foster

Howard Palmer

George K. Jarvis

UTAH STATE UNIVERSITY PRESS
1990

First published in the United States by
Utah State University Press
Logan, Utah 84322-7800

ISBN 0-87421-147-6

Copyright © The University of Alberta Press 1990

First published in Canada by
The University of Alberta Press, Edmonton, Alberta

**Library of Congress Cataloging-in-Publication Data**

The Mormon presence in Canada / edited by Brigham Y. Card . . . [et al.].
   p.  cm.
  Papers presented at a conference held at the University of Alberta,
Edmonton, May 6-9, 1987.
  Includes bibliographical references.
  ISBN 0-87421-147-6 : $30.00
  1. Mormons—Canada—History—Congresses. 2. Canada—Church
history—Congresses. 3. Sociology, Christian (Mormon)—Congresses.
4. Canada—Emigration and immigration—History—Congresses.
5. United States—Emigration and immigration—History—Congresses.
I. Card. B. Y. (Brigham Young), 1914-
F1035.M67M66  1990
971'.0088283—dc20                  90-34484
                                        CIP

The paper used in this publication meets the minimum requirements of the
American National Standards for Permanence of Paper for Printed Library
Materials, Z39.48-1984. ∞

Typesetting by Pièce de Résistance Ltée., Edmonton, Alberta, Canada

Printed by Gagné Printing Ltd., Louiseville, Quebec, Canada

# AMERICAN ACTRESS
## Perspective
## on the
## Nineteenth
## Century

CLAUDIA D. JOHNSON

NELSON-HALL nh
CHICAGO

Excerpts from *Troupers of the Gold Coast or the Rise of Lotta Crabtree* by Constance Rourke, copyright 1928 by Harcourt Brace Jovanovich, Inc.; renewed 1956 by Alice D. Fore. Reprinted by permission of the publisher.

LIBRARY OF CONGRESS CATALOGING IN PUBLICATION DATA

Johnson, Claudia D.
   American Actress.

   Bibliography: p.
   Includes index.
   1. Actresses—United States—Biography.   2. Theater—
United States—History—19th century.   I. Title.
PN2285.J64 1984       792'.028'0922 [B]        84-6867
ISBN 0-8304-1026-0

PN
2285
J64
1984

*In memory of Jim Durst*

# CONTENTS

# ACKNOWLEDGMENTS

For research assistance, manuscript preparation, and funding I owe special debts to Catherine Jones, Karen Nelson, Crystel Bell, Eleanor Tubbs, and the Research Grants Committee of The University of Alabama. For research assistance as well as permission to use photographs, I am grateful to the Harvard Theater Collection, the Albert and Victoria Museum, the Boston Public Library, the Library of Congress, and Columbia University Press.

Most of all, I thank Vernon Johnson for all kinds of expert and generously given help.

# AMERICAN ACTRESS

# *ENTER THE HARLOT*

On the sixth of September in 1857, two women, one middle aged, the other about sixty-three, lay in the receiving tomb of Greenwood Cemetery in New York City. The certificate of burial identified the younger woman as Mrs. Matilda I. Reillieux. The older was entered on the certificate only as "& co." Both women were eventually buried in the same grave, the identity of the older woman still a mystery. The tombstone finally erected over the grave bore only these words: "My Mother and Grandmother." A dark secret so tainted the older woman that she was buried without a name on her grave. Yet no debauched and criminal personal life had in old age prompted her to keep her identity a secret during her last years and later to cause her relatives to bury her identity with her bones; everyone who had known her testified to her impeccable life as a faithful and self-sacrificing wife and a loving mother of ten children. The "dishonor" of this woman, finally identified as Mary Ann Duff, lay elsewhere: for twenty-eight years, until she was forty-four years old, she had been an actress on the American stage. Moreover, she had been the first great tragedienne of the American theater, praised by Edwin Booth as the greatest tragic actress in the world.

The shame that Mary Ann Duff felt about her former profession and her successful attempts to bury her past are entirely predictable in light of her

"Where is your home?" "Where mother is." (Martha Louise Rayne, *What Can a Woman Do?*)

3

conversion in middle age to a straight-and-narrow sectarian life, for religious Americans in a church-centered country were far from friendly toward the theater. The American actress in the nineteenth century was a member of a profession that historically had been outlawed with some frequency, its members officially labeled vagabonds and, from the time of the Tudors, considered déclassé. In the United States, in her own time, the stigma attached to the nineteenth-century actress's profession was doubly strong because of the arm of New England Puritanism, still reaching out of its own grave, and because of the inordinate power of the Protestant church which had flatly declared the theater, with its illusion, emotion, and sensuality, to be the enemy of all religion. The theatrical community's competition with the church for the attention, time, and money of the public, and the stage's ancient association with strong drink and prostitution, worked counter to the church and to many social reforms in an age of reformation. In the eyes of many Americans, it also posed a constant threat to the sacred American home, to its fireside angel, the ideal American mother, and to the very fabric of the nation. The continual branding of the actress as a pernicious temptress in a circle of bad magic meant that frequent social ostracism and constant clerical excoriation were a part of her way of life.

An episode in the life of another nineteenth-century actress illustrates the ironic force of anti-theatrical attitudes. Clara Morris's mother, who had struggled all her adult life in the most menial and demeaning of domestic positions, as housekeeper and seamstress, was "stricken with horror" when her daughter turned to the theater as the only likely means of sharing the family's financial burden.[1] The episode illustrates the ambiguity of the actress's position: she was able to anticipate professional rewards which few other women in the age enjoyed, but only at considerable sacrifice of intangibles precious to nineteenth-century woman—personal esteem and social acceptability.

In the eighteenth century, when theatrical companies began making their appearance on the American scene, an actor was as likely to be arrested as applauded in many parts of the country—the fate of a company of comedians who attempted to entertain the Philadelphians in 1749.[2] Theater was banned rather than encouraged in places where the colonists strictly practiced their religion. The Quakers in Pennsylvania and the Calvinists in New England were noted for their stringency in prohibiting players. William Dunlap, that pioneer and historian of the American stage, claimed that southern towns (one thinks of Richmond and Charleston), being largely Episcopalian in colonial days, were more tolerant.[3] Although theater had already appeared in the New World before 1774, in that year the Provincial Congress passed a resolution discouraging public amusements, including theater—not just in New England, but everywhere in the colonies. This recommendation lost its force during the Revolutionary War, but prohibitions of and protests against the stage continued to reveal the displeasure of a large portion of the public.

Even after the Revolution, when the theater was legal in New York City, objections continued to be raised, not just on religious, but on socioeconomic and national grounds: patriots argued that it was wrong for those with money to squander it on trifling amusements while the nation and the nation's needy wanted the bare necessities.[4] In 1786 seven hundred New York citizens asked without success for an immediate suppression of the theater.[5] The sons of the Puritans staunchly held firm against the theater in Massachusetts until 1793, when the ban against public entertainments was finally lifted.[6]

After 1800 religious institutions in America were no longer capable of legislating wide-scale legal prohibitions of the theater, but until the last decades of the century, their opposition had as much forceful conviction behind it as it ever had. Because the Protestant church was admittedly the principal opponent of the theater, the position of the actress and her profession must be regarded in light of the church's status in the nineteenth century.

Despite the country's earlier abandonment of a state religion and the clear constitutional separation of church and state, Protestant churches in particular grew to be uncommonly forceful during the century as the result of numerous events, including the Second Great Awakening and the waves of revivals which continually swept the country. The many sects, though independent and diverse, were strong. As Sidney E. Ahlstrom wrote in *The Religious History of the American People,* "Despite the legal separation of church and state, this American Protestant mainstream would enjoy the influence and self-confidence of a formal establishment."[7] Firsthand observations by Englishmen and Europeans bear this out. As early as 1835 Alexis de Tocqueville noted the same anomaly—that an unofficial institution could become very powerful and pervade so many diverse segments of American life:

> Religion in America takes no direct part in the government of society, but nevertheless it must be regarded as the foremost of the political institutions

of that country. . . . I do not know whether all the Americans have a sincere faith in their religion, for who can search the human heart? But I am certain that they hold it to be indispensable to the maintenance of republican institutions. This opinion is not peculiar to a class of citizens or to a party, but it belongs to the whole nation, and to every rank of society.[8]

Later travelers, like Thomas Colley Grattan, who observed American society in 1859, were impressed with the sheer numbers of people and the intensity of activity in American churches:

In no country of the world is there more religious fervour, than in America, and nowhere a more strict observance of forms. The true religious sentiment, that has its source and life in the hearts of men, is out of the pale of calculation; but the numerical force of observers of church discipline, in all its varieties, is, I have no doubt, greater in the United States than anywhere else.[9]

Grattan's impressions were certainly accurate, because Protestantism had grown by leaps and bounds in the first half of the century. Between 1800 and 1850, membership in Protestant churches increased "ten fold."[10] According to one estimate, the 40 percent of the population who were church members in 1800 had risen to 75 percent by 1835.[11]

Even this high percentage of church members probably fails to reflect the real impact of the church on the population, because almost three times as many people attended church as joined it. The churches' mastery over the public was facilitated by the high esteem in which the clergy were held. The always critical Mrs. Frances Trollope would even argue that the clergy had assumed inordinate power, had woven an unwholesome spell over the public. Once you had joined a sect in America, she wrote, "your next submission must be that of unqualified obedience to the will and pleasure of your elected pastor."[12] The opinions of the clergy were made known, not only from the pulpit on Sunday, but through the organizing of religious education classes, prayer meetings, and charity and missionary gatherings of all kinds which occupied much of the churchgoers' time. Mrs. Trollope reported that "every evening that is not spent in the churches and meeting houses, is devoted to what would be called parties by others, but which they designate as prayer meetings."[13] Church opinion was also transmitted through a rapidly growing religious press, which outstripped the secular press from 1840 to 1860 and was "widely and avidly read."[14]

The Reverend G. Lewis, a Scottish observer of American churches, noticed this marvel in 1848; "everything connected with a congregation," he wrote, "is reported through the religious press."[15]

Ironically enough, then, the "voluntary" church of the United States grew in numbers, energy, reputation, and influence as revivals sprang up, particularly in rural areas along the frontier, as the social life of the ordinary American came to center on the church, as ministerial "stars" like Charles G. Finney and Henry Ward Beecher commanded public attention, and as sectarian publishing houses and periodicals proliferated. As Winthrop S. Hudson concluded, Protestantism

> had established undisputed sway over almost all aspects of the national life. It was a Protestant America that had been fashioned by the churches; and the influence of the churches . . . extended far beyond their somewhat narrowly defined membership. The vast majority of Americans, even when not actual communicants, regarded themselves as "adherents" of one church or another; and among the populace at large the patterns of belief and conduct—both private and public, individual and corporate—were set by the churches.[16]

The American clergy seem to have pooled these vast resources to speak with one loud voice against what they agreed was tantamount to the anti-Christ—the villainous, ubiquitous theater. Virtually every Protestant sect in America, with the sole exception of the Episcopal church, officially and unequivocally declared the theater to be the haunt of sinners. Presbyterians, Congregationalists, Baptists, Methodists, and Quakers—north, south, east, and west—if they agreed on nothing else, agreed on this.[17] Prominent clergymen of every denomination aimed their most torrid rhetoric at the theater, calling it a den of Satan to be avoided at all costs. Many of them agreed with Timothy Dwight, president of Yale College and a nationally known theologian, who wrote that theater people were "a nuisance in the earth, the very offal of society."[18] Other leading ministers of the century, including Lyman and Henry Ward Beecher and Dwight L. Moody, raved against the theater as it it were the black plague. Henry Ward Beecher, whose much-publicized trial for adultery only dented his charisma, called the theater "the gate of debauchery, the porch of pollution . . . the door to all the sinks of iniquity."[19]

The intensity of conviction about the theater can be found in many sermons, which burn with the extreme language of the Reverend Robert Hatfield and the Reverend DeWitt Talmadge, who believed that young men and women would be better off dead than in even the briefest association with actors. Hatfield put his case in what he obviously regarded as a rhetorical question: "Let me ask you, my young friend, justly proud of your sister, would you not rather follow her to her grave tonight than to know that tomorrow she shall stand at the altar and pledge her faith and trust her precious future to an actor?"[20] The Reverend Talmadge, who in the 1870s officiated over the largest church congregation in New York, declared that most people would rather see their children "five feet under the ground of Greenwood" than "in a month's association with actors."[21] The Reverend Herrick Johnson raised the specter of a fate even worse than the pro- verbial sister's marriage to an actor: "How many young men of clean pure homes care to have their sisters tread the boards?"[22] Again the answer is obvious: none! It would be an unthinkable abhorrence, as Talmadge implied in another of his dramatic questions: "Why is it, when you speak of a woman's attachment to the stage, you speak of it in a whisper, saying, 'She is an actress!'"[23]

The conflict between church and stage was not merely rhetorical. Testimony survives describing open hostility on many occasions be- tween actors and the churchgoing public. Several successful managers— William Wood, Sol Smith, and Noah Ludlow—harbored no little bitterness about the church's antipathy toward actors and thought it of sufficient importance to record in their memoirs. Wood, a manager who worked throughout the northeast, recounted an incident that took place in Baltimore in 1816, just after his company had opened with a production of *Bertram*—a play that was not expected to enrage the church because it had been written by a minister and edited and approved by English censors. Despite clerical attacks on the play as immoral, Wood decided to produce it and cast his wife, the company's leading lady, in the starring role. On the Sunday following the per- formance, an unnamed minister in the city made a special point of attacking both the play and the leading lady who, as it turned out, was one of his faithful parishioners:

On one occasion the speaker became so much carried away by a mistaken impression, as boldly to appeal to his audience, and ask what estimate could anyone make of the feelings or the principles of that woman—of her perceptions of right and wrong—who could be found capable of repre- senting the heroine of this shameful production. I know not whether the gentleman was aware that the unfortunate person who the week before, in discharge of her professional engagements, had been representing this character, was at the very time a regular member of his own congregation, and was seated on that Sunday, as she usually was, in her accustomed place at church. . . .[24]

The frontier, less tradition bound and less religious, might be expected to be less biased against the theater, but actors met with disfavor even there. Noah Ludlow, managing a company in the frontier Midwest and South, attested to the same conflict in his memoirs. The tone he adopted in referring to the vilification of actors by the clergy is unmistakably bitter. His fellow actors, he said, had been "stigmatized" by the church; the churchgoing public had been brainwashed by the clergy, like one in Ohio in 1828:

> No attraction could bring together a succession of full houses in a city where many persons were afraid to go to a theater, lest they should be "talked about" by those who were members of churches where the clergy were continually consigning *actors* and those who supported them to the *Infernal* regions.[25]

Sol Smith, who later, in 1835, became Ludlow's partner, was having similar trouble with the clergy in the same season while he was playing in Alabama:

> The preachers carried the day and the *night* too, and we were very glad to escape without a serious pecuniary loss. Yet our performances were not without their moral effect, though the preachers endeavored to make their hearers believe that all who visited the theater would certainly be eternally roasted in the hottest sort of fires, the heat of which were to be intensified by liberal supplies of brimstone![26]

The fragmentary notebooks of a minor traveling actor named H. Watkins yield two examples of the actor's awareness of church hostility. The first is the account of a touring company that was unable to get a decent funeral for one of its deceased actors in Ohio in the 1840s:

> They went to a priest to pray for him, but he would neither pray nor allow him to be buried in Catholic ground, so they got a Universalist preacher, who in his *sermon* took upon himself to slander members of the profession.[27]

Being again unable to secure a minister for an actor's funeral in New Orleans, the company's manager, Sol Smith, had to officiate:

Having no minister, Sol Smith officiated. He spoke very feelingly, and
with more sincerity than a minister would, for the latter would undoubtedly
have slandered the profession.[28]

The most notorious example of clerical prejudice against actors, cited
by Ludlow, Joseph Jefferson, and others, occurred in 1870 in New
York City at the death of a famous and well-loved comedian, George
Holland. Jefferson, an exceptionally reputable actor, accompanied Holland's son to make arrangements for the funeral, but when the Reverend
Dr. Lorenzo Sabine, an Episcopalian minister, heard that the deceased
had been an actor, he refused to allow the funeral in his church.[29]
Jefferson found the ordeal intensely humiliating, especially in the presence of Holland's son. It was not, however, a surprise to him, because
when his own actor grandfather had been buried in 1832, the officiating
minister had refused to say the words, "our deceased brother," which
belonged in the ceremony. Instead he substituted, as an exception in
the case of an actor, the words, "this man."[30]

In trying to assess the value of these clerical views in determining
that larger climate of opinion with which the actress had to contend,
one has, of course, to acknowledge that the church constituted only
one of many voices in a large nation. Nevertheless, the voice of the
church was a loud and strident one to which many people listened as
if their souls depended on it. Just how much of the general public
actually did hold the same low view of the theater and actors as did
the clergy would be difficult to determine, but one can certainly con-
clude that many people living in nineteenth-century America *believed*
that the general public held the same opinion. John Hodgkinson, for
example, an actor-manager and contemporary of William Dunlap,
referred to opinions held by the general populace, not just the clergy,
in writing of the actor's station at the turn of the nineteenth century:

The situation of a Theatrical Performer seems here to be peculiarly unfortunate: Strong Prejudices are entertained against the Profession, and against
the Drama itself by many . . . and so wide is the Prepossession against
the Calling, that *many* look upon an actor as something different from his
fellow Men.[31]

Four decades later, Philip Hone, mayor of New York City from
1825 to 1826, also wrote of a public—not solely a clerical—sentiment
in recording that "the stage is indiscriminately voted immoral, irre-

ligious and, what is much worse, *unfashionable.*"[32] No act of his public life cost him so much political support, he claimed, as when he extended the dignity of his office to the new Bowery Theater by appearing and speaking at its opening in 1832.[33] Both Mrs. Trollope in 1827 and J. S. Buckingham in the 1840s concluded that the general public did not approve of theatrical exhibitions.[34] Albert M. Palmer, one of the most successful theater owners and managers in the last half of the century, estimated that at least until mid-century, seven-tenths of the population looked on stage attendance as "almost a sin." He observed some improvement in the public's attitude toward the profession by the 1880s and 1890s.[35] Daniel Frohman, another outstanding producer of the period, known as the "star maker," corroborated Palmer's conclusion that as late as the 1860s antitheatrical bias was far reaching: "Within my memory, playgoing had been considered unethical not only by the clergy, but by church-goers."[36]

There is no denying the fact that good actresses received the plaudits of the play-going public in the nineteenth century, and that occasionally some of them even came into contact with genteel society, but they were also aware that such occasions were exceptional and that their professional success was quite another thing from social success. All the plaudits in the world did not alter the general public's view of actresses as a "low order of society," a classless group of people "very properly debarred from respectable society."[37] Anna Cora Mowatt, an actress born into wealth and prestige, recognized "the prejudices of the world against the profession as a body."[38] The actor, she wrote, dwells "on the outer side of a certain conventional pale of society, which he is allowed to enter only by courtesy, unless it is broken through by the majesty of transcendent talents."[39] Clara Morris, born and reared at the opposite, lowest end of the social spectrum from Mowatt, reached the same conclusion—that members of her profession had labored under a cloud of disapproval throughout most of her career, which had begun in the 1860s: "Even the people who did not think all actors drunkards and all actresses immoral did think they were a lot of flighty, silly buffoons, not to be taken seriously for a moment."[40] Although the cloud of public suspicion was slowly lifting during the last decades of the century, Morris left no doubt about having felt its presence in the 1860s: "The actor had no social standing; he was no longer looked down upon, but he was an unknown quantity."[41] By the 1880s and 1890s, she believed that some members of the profession had "won some social recognition."[42]

Sol Smith, who repeatedly defended his profession against attack, as he did in the following answer to a sermon by Lyman Beecher, epitomized the antipathy between two cultural polarities: the highly esteemed religious establishment and Smith's own profession, whose members were often social outcasts:

> *You* are a preacher of the Gospel; *I* am nothing but an actor, and a *poor* one at that. . . . I may add that *you* stand at the head of a powerful sect of professing Christians in the United States, while *I* am content to claim membership in the lowest rank of artists called histrions. I presume, if I were to seek a conversation with you at your splendid mansion, I should be spurned from your door as unworthy to press your carpet with my unhallowed feet. The name of "Sol Smith, the actor," announced in your study, would probably be the signal for bolting your doors. [43]

Of course, there are paradoxes and qualifications to be considered in judging the public view of the actress and her profession: the theater did show an overall growth in the century, and many plays were well attended; many actresses were very well received professionally; many were entertained socially by gentlemen, and a few were even privy to polite female society. The whole status of the profession began gradually to improve from the 1860s onward.

For a variety of reasons the last decades of the century saw an abatement of the religious public's disapproval of the theater. One reason seems to have been that theaters had proven their ability to work for moral causes. *The Drunkard,* produced by P. T. Barnum in 1844, had clearly been an effective weapon against Demon Rum in the minds of some people. Women who had never darkened the door of a theater had come and brought their husbands, some of whom were presumably likely candidates for reform. [44] Although Harriet Beecher Stowe had refused to stage *Uncle Tom's Cabin* because she was afraid it would draw people into the theater and encourage a theater-going habit, the story reached the stage with great success and is credited with having improved the tone of the theater. [45] Another reason for the abatement of the hostilities between theater and church is that most legitimate theaters had closed the bars and the gathering places for prostitutes within their walls. Also to be considered is the church's waning influence over the public—the clerical power that had been used as a weapon against the theater was on the decline anyhow. [46]

The reasons for the reputation of actresses in the century are many and complex and not altogether unique to the time and place. However, at least part of the reason can be attributed to the fact that the theater—as it was in reality and as it was *imagined* to be—ran against the grain of American society at large. Here was an age that cherished above all things the vision of an ideal world dominated by the ideal family supported by the church. Against these domestic and religious standards, other entities in society, including the theater, were measured. It was an age that idealized womanhood as well, and measured all women, including the actress, against the ideal. In the minds of many people, the theater miserably failed in that comparison; at the worst it was considered one of the most formidable enemies of home and ideal womanhood—those sacrosanct institutions on which rested personal salvation, financial success, and national survival.[47] In the wake of a century rife with upheaval and turbulence, the home was both teacher and stabilizer. Before the hearth, family members learned moral virtues and religious truths, invaluable not only to their own souls but to the well-being of society. If family life disintegrated, the result for the community might be crime, indolence, and rebellion; eventually, the nation, itself an extended family, would fall.

The values of nineteenth-century society were those that grew from and strengthened the family: fidelity, to protect the union of husband and wife; duty, to preserve the bonds between parent and child; respect for and acceptance of the traditionally assigned places of wife, husband, and children; reason and moderation, to encourage virtue and order.[48] Individuals and other social institutions that reflected these domestic values were beneficial; those associated with opposing values—adventuresomeness, rebellion, excitement, and unconventionality—were deemed to be injurious to the home and the family and, therefore, to be avoided.

A sizable proportion of the population branded the theater "bad" because the nature of the audience and the plays themselves were believed to undermine family life. In this regard, the most convincing argument, one which theatrical people could scarcely refute, was the friendly alliance between the stage and prostitutes. Although numerous actors and managers lamented this association, it was the presence of prostitutes in the theater's audiences which, more than any one thing, seemed to besmirch the actor's reputation.[49] There were a few theaters which occasionally operated without reserving their third tiers for prostitutes, but records indicate that most theaters from east to west, north to south, perpetuated the practice.[50] Even in its infancy American theater had extended its hospitality to prostitutes by reserving an upper tier, often called the gallery, to ladies of the evening.[51] Here they attracted the attention of prospective customers who, as a rule, accompanied them to less public, more disreputable houses, a practice which earned the theater the dramatic epithet of "a place of assignation."[52] In a few cases the gallery was more than just a "place of assignation"; the prostitutes and their clients began and completed their transactions in the gallery, according to John Murtagh and Sara Harris in their study of prostitution: "Prostitutes were among the theater's most ardent habitues. They swarmed the galleries, using them not only for purposes of pick up, but also as places where their relations with unfinicky customers could be consummated."[53] Often prostitutes could and did assume a proprietary air in the theater, and with good cause—their presence was frequently solicited by the management with free passes, often delivered to houses of ill repute on the day before a performance.[54]

> Free admissions are now being dispensed to the public courtezans of the town, in order that their vile paramours may be induced to follow them, whereby the receipts of the house may be nightly increased; and the profits of the lessees of the saloons are greatly enhanced in consequence of the greater demand for their various species of intoxicating beverage.[55]

Obviously, many managers depended as much on the drawing power of the prostitutes as they did the play, fearing that their establishments could not endure without third-tier patronage, a point of view eagerly

Queen of the family. (L. P. Brockett, *Woman: Her Rights, Wrongs, Privileges, and Responsibilities*)

adopted by detractors who were convinced that the theater was beyond redemption because it had inevitably to lean upon "vice." A number of theaters, notably Boston's Tremont, did close down for good after abolishing the third tier. One manager, Edmund Simpson of New York's Park Theater, cut short an experiment of closing off the tier in 1842 when he found the departure from custom to be disastrous for business.[56] Noah Ludlow had better success in closing his Mobile Theater to prostitutes, although it was not done with impunity:

> I had a hard struggle for this scheme of reformation. . . . From time to time, for some two or three years following my management in St. Louis and Mobile, and in subsequent years in New Orleans, I had sent to me through the post-office threatening missives, such as "cowhidings," "fisticuffings," and "shootings," and the like, for refusing admission to these *filles de joie*; but persisted in my course and finally gained my point.[57]

It would be next to impossible to pinpoint the exact day when the very last third tier was closed, but it is safe to assume that the custom had largely disappeared by the 1870s. Of course, the third tier was only the most infamous part of the theater. Other portions of the house had also been frequented by prostitutes, along with regular patrons. So, although the closing of the tier modified the theater's official alliance with prostitutes, it did not drive them out altogether but simply relocated them to other parts of the house. In fact, some people believed that failure to segregate prostitutes by providing them with their own tier would produce an even worse situation. The *New York Morning Herald* in 1838 insisted that the Park provide a separate entrance along with the separate tier to keep prostitutes from mixing with respectable patrons:

> On Friday night the Park Theatre contained 83 of the most profligate and abandoned women that ever disgraced humanity; they entered in the same door, and for a time mixed indiscriminately with 63 virtuous and respectable ladies. . . . Men of New York, take not your wives and daughters to the Park Theatre, until Mr. Simpson pays some respect to them by constructing a separate entrance for the abandoned of the sex.[58]

Needless to say, the nineteenth-century individual believed that the theater's prostitutes constituted an appalling threat to the home and family.[59] Fallen women bewitched both husbands and sons away from home and led them down the road to misery and ruin. As the Reverend

Talmadge wrote, "Husbands who have lost all love for home go there."[60] Olive Logan, herself an actress, believed that "many a parent has learned from sad experience that he was in error when he permitted his children to visit places of amusement where free license was given to prostitutes."[61] The damage to the family was often paramount in the minds of those who spoke and wrote against the theater's third tier: "Why is it that the streets and lanes leading to every haunt of infamy in the city resound nightly to wheels passing to and from the Theatre; and why is it that so many heart-broken mothers and grief-stricken sisters mourn hopelessly over their profligate sons and brothers?"[62] Another tract against the theater reports the despair of a mother over her imprisoned son who has been led astray by the theater. "O that theatre! He was a virtuous, kind youth; til that theatre proved his ruin."[63] One of the most melodramatic stories, repeatedly used in tracts against the stage, is about a once-innocent young man who died from pneumonia after falling into a canal while in pursuit of a prostitute named Emily. The story of his ruin, told on his deathbed, was broadcast by the religious press:

> "It would tire you to relate how I was first enticed to go upstairs into the splendid saloon, then to the third tier, where the prostitutes are allotted a place. One night, the most fascinating amongst them, Emily was her name, came up to me, and took my arm. I had not the power to resist the temptor, and was persuaded to accompany her to her brothel."[64]

The theater prostitute was frequently spoken of as infecting the home metaphorically, but there was, of course, a very real fear of literal infection as well. One of the greatest anxieties of the nineteenth-century wife was the fear of being infected by her husband with venereal disease.[65] Dr. William Sanger, physician at the Blackwell Island Hospital, who in 1859 published his study of the prostitutes arrested in New York City, found that many of the lowest class of prostitutes frequented theaters.[66] Seventy-five thousand of them received treatment for venereal disease each year. Two of every five came to him for treatment, and he commented that "if only half were so suffering, and each of these infected only one man, the result would be 365,000 men diseased each year."[67]

Probably far more real damage was thought to be wreaked upon the home by another of the theater's demons—Demon Rum. For the first half of the century, a bar was attached to the third tier so that the usual rowdy tendencies of "the gallery gods" were exacerbated by imbibing strong drink. Murtagh and Harris reported an observation by a British visitor in 1830: "There is not a dance hall, a free-and-easy, a concert saloon, or a vile drinking place that presents such a view of the depravity and degradation of New York as the gallery of a Bowery theatre."[68] The bar, of course, was always seen as contributing to that depravity, and rarely does an attack on the theater fail to mention the presence of this abomination.[69] If the bar was not good for the theater's reputation, however, it was, like the third tier, important for the theater's economy. The inevitable losses in the presentation of a play could usually be recouped in the bar; so the enemies of the theater could claim with some justification that the bar underwrote the theater.[70]

Unfortunately for the good name of the theater in the nineteenth century, at the same time that the operation of drinking establishments was customary, sympathy for temperance and abstinence was exceedingly strong. Drunkenness was believed to be at the bottom of every hideous crime and disgusting failing that undermined the home and the country, according to J. C. Furnas in *The Americans:* "On the face of it, poverty, prostitution, fornication-*cum*-bastardy, homicide, insanity, malnutrition, political corruption, damnation—for drunkenness erodes integrity, and St. Paul listed drunkards with numerous murderers and sodomites as ineligible for salvation—all were intimates of Demon Rum."[71]

The strongly held notion that the bar was the family's enemy is implied by the large numbers of married women who joined the cause of temperance and provided it with its fierce momentum,[72] culminating at one stage in the Women's Crusade, when hundreds of women throughout the Midwest and Northeast marched on the saloons to close what they considered to be the source of alcoholism and drunkenness of their own husbands or the husbands of their friends.[73] The history of temperance in the nineteenth century reveals that many women, and middle-class businessmen as well, perceived taverns and bars to be among the most vicious enemies of the American home and the American way of life,[74] and theaters became known as home wreckers by virtue of their customary maintenance of bars in various parts of the house. It was supposed that in the theater's bar, the defenses of the young, inexperienced man were broken down, making him fair game for the third-tier prostitutes. There, the money meant to put food in the mouths of babes was thrown away on whiskey. There the weak and foolish husband fed a craving that would lead him and his family down the road to ruin: "driven from business, excluded from virtuous society, divorced from his broken-hearted wife, deserted by all his friends."[75] Clergymen claimed that many married women believed that the drink served in the theater's bars had destroyed their homes.[76]

During the last half of the century, many cities and towns passed laws to prohibit theatrical bars, like New York's Concert Hall Act of 1862. The subsequent failure of many small theaters proved to attackers of the theater that connections between the stage and vice were too vital to be severed. The result of the Concert Hall Act was the creation of "concert saloons" which circumvented the law by eliminating the curtain.[77] Because a hall with no curtain was not technically considered a theater, liquor could be served, even though entertainments, including plays, were presented. By 1869, for example, six hundred concert saloons operated in New York City.[78] Thus, many theaters remained "tainted," not only with prostitutes but with bars, even after the third tier and the bar were "officially" closed.

Both classic and modern plays were found to be sacriligious, immoral, and false. Shakespeare's comedies were lewd, therefore unacceptable. His tragedies had no moral messages. One minister leveled particular complaints against *Hamlet's* failure as a moral drama: Polonius's wise advice, he charged, is ridiculed; the only really good character, Ophelia, is shown as impossibly weak and demented; and King Claudius, as wicked as he is, is allowed to keel right over without any real physical suffering.[79] A Baptist minister, the Reverend Jeremiah Jeter, afforded Shakespeare the benefit of a strange doubt in attacking his plays: "For the honor of his genius, I am willing to believe that Shakespeare was not the author of the profane and obscene language in his plays."[80]

Far too many plays, both old and new, portrayed vice of all kinds, presented loose women and licentious men in a sympathetic or comical light, and mocked ministers or religion in general. The Reverend James Monroe Buckeley analyzed popular plays in typical fashion. He disparaged *She Stoops to Conquer* as an example of "profaneness" and "vulgarity," a play which "sneers at temperance and religion."[81] *School for Scandal*, also frequently chosen for production, he called a play that "no woman could read to any but her husband, or some other near relative, without giving grounds for a presumption against her purity."[82] *The Ticket of Leave Man*, another popular play, was to be avoided because it presented "scenes of vice" and "coarseness."[83] The play *Saratoga*, was "unchaste" and pervaded with *double entendre*. Finally, he attacks *East Lynne* as a typical example of the theater's sympathetic

treatment of such evils as adultery, infidelity, and murder.[84] Few plays
escaped without criticism of some kind. Buckley also disapproved of
the use of "slang" and portrayals of remarriage. Another minister even
objected to plays that showed dueling.[85]

Even should a play show a triumph of virtue over vice, its portrayal
was often reproachable:

> It is true, villainy is commonly punished in these plays, but the villainy
> is often given such dash and daring and bravado, and is so set round with
> attractions and is pursued with such utter abandon and intoxication of
> delight that many a youth is led to prefer the way to destruction and the
> devil; because the journey can be made in such a blaze of glory.[86]

Women were, presumably, more likely to be led astray by dramas
than were men, who were more occupied with activities in the audience:

> A mother might fear the polluting comedy for her son but the more
> absorbing tragedy for her daughter. Pride, ambition, and revenge, lust,
> seduction, and murder are, I need not tell you, the materials of which the
> tragedy is composed; and it is not to be imagined that the delicate mind
> of a female, young and imaginative as she may be, can be agitated by
> scenes like these . . . and yet suffer no depravation.[87]

Naturally, viewing plays took up time that a woman should more
properly have been devoting to her household duties,[88] but the danger
in the theater for women was more serious than this. Theatergoing
was feared as an addiction very like the addiction to heroin or alcohol:
once having gotten a good taste of theatrical productions, a person
would find it almost impossible to give them up. Clergymen believed
that the theater addict would do almost anything to satisfy his or her
habit. Policemen cited instances of boys being led to the gallows as a
result of their criminal search for money to see plays, as well as stories
of men dying sad, premature deaths from dissipations brought on by
viewing plays. As drastic as these cases sounded, the extremes to which
play addiction led the average man were not believed to be nearly so
disastrous as those that awaited women: for the price of a theater ticket,
poor men pilfered and stole. Women, however, had poor-paying jobs,
or no jobs, to support their habit, and it was believed that they were
led to prostitution for the price of a theater ticket. This is the warning
of a Professor Griscom that was frequently quoted in tracts and newspaper columns:

In the case of the feebler sex, the result is still worse; a relish for the amusements of the theater, without the means of indulgence, becomes too often a motive for listening to the first seducer; and this prepares the unfortunate captive of sensuality for the haunts of infamy and a total destruction of all that is valuable in the mind and character of woman.[89]

Another alarmist argued along the same lines: "The excitement produced by the theater's attractive introduction to the female mind of licentiousness and her eagerness—addiction to it—for which money is necessary, starts many a young woman toward the fall."[90]

The wife, that moral rock of the American home, might become dissatisfied with her life as she witnessed a play, realizing that her own quiet home was dull compared to that of the characters she saw on stage. Even if she were not provoked to desert her home, even if a young daughter did not resort to prostitution to support her habit of theatergoing, woman's awakening to her own dull lot, as a result of seeing plays, was not deemed likely to strengthen the ideal home. Women as well as men could develop a "distaste for simple and home-born enjoyments, as well as for sober everyday duties!"[91] In short, "the sweet charities of home will lose their attraction. Ordinary scenes of social joy and fireside satisfactions will be exchanged for resorts of more tumultuous excitement."[92]

Very little good of any kind could come of the "tumultuous excitement" so easily provoked by the theater. Indeed, the domestic virtues were not exciting ones, but quiet ones, just the opposite of theatrical attributes. So the home promoted one set of values, and the theater elevated quite another set. In the cause of personal morality and social order, home was the place where the "highest" faculties were to be fortified, and those included reason, resolution, moderation, harmony, simplicity, tranquility, and dedication to duty.[93] These admirable qualities all helped to keep in check those opposite, dangerous faculties that led to personal and national ruin. The distinct tone of the ideal home is suggested by the many adjectives used by nineteenth-century Americans to describe it: soothing, refining, peaceful, serene, composed, regular, controlled, serious, decorous, austere.[94] To promote these virtues, the ideal home was run on a rigid schedule, children were disciplined to be respectful and orderly, the "grosser nature" of the men in the family was refined, and the simple home entertainments such as reading were encouraged.[95]

The opposing faculties which the home was expected to moderate were passion, wild imagination, sensuality, and excesses of all kinds.

A gentleman, writing advice to his sister in 1850, for example, admonished her to "keep a constant watch over the imagination . . . since this is the medium through which temptation comes, never suffer your fancy to rove without control."[96] Arguments presented against playgoing invariably warned against the dangers of these pernicious faculties, which were excited by the theater. It was by nature a place of excess and turbulence. The atmosphere of the pit and the third tier encouraged overt sexuality, rowdiness, even violence.

Washington Irving was one of the earliest recorders of the excessive rowdiness in American theaters. Just after the turn of the century, he wrote of Jonathan Oldstyle being hit in the head with "a rotten pippin" thrown from the gallery and of a stranger near him being hit with an apple.[97] George C. D. Odell recorded numerous instances in New York in the 1820s when the stage was bombarded with food, and Judge C.H. Haswell, another firsthand observer of New York theaters between 1816 and 1860, remembered that, after suppers were consumed in the upper circles of theaters, the leavings were usually aimed at the heads of the patrons in the pit.[98] Mrs. Trollope, the most graphic exposer of American behavior in the theater, was repulsed by the constant yelling, throwing, and spitting even in fashionable parts of midwestern and eastern theaters. On one occasion she was shocked beyond belief to see a man have a violent fit of vomiting in the theater and even more amazed to observe that the other members of the audience treated it as a normal occurrence.[99] Conditions among southern audiences seem to have been much the same. W. Stanley Hoole, in his history *The Ante-Bellum Charleston Theater,* mentioned constant complaints from the public about the yelling, spitting, picking of pockets, drunkenness, and brawls in the audiences.[100] What Maria Child observed in the Bowery was representative of many theater nights all over the country: the pit patrons, she writes, "get up a gratuitous battle, more lively than those on stage."[101]

Very often the theater was not just noisy and dirty, it was violent, and that widespread violence, particularly in the first half of the century, was the epitome of the excessive passion from which the home sought to shield its members. One such violent occasion, a riot provoked by a disgruntled actor who had departed the company, was described by William Wood. On the first night of a performance in this 1811-12 season, the audience began hurling missiles of all sorts onto the stage and yelling, "Kill him! Kill him!" On the second night, the disturbance reached riot proportions when the leading lady, Mrs.

Rowdiness: The Bowery Theatre. (Harvard Theatre Collection)

Wood, was hit by a musket ball that had been thrown on the stage. Wood, the manager, was pursued through the streets by a mob from the theater, until rescued by a Good Samaritan.[102] Another riot in 1825 was excited by the performance of Edmund Kean, an Englishman appearing on stage at a time of high nationalistic fervor. No one was hurt, but the damage to the building itself was considerable:

> The pit was soon cleared, and benches, lamps, and almost everything that could be moved were thrown into the pit. Many of the windows were destroyed, the doors broken, the front of the gallery and boxes were injured, and the chandeliers broken to atoms.[103]

The "Anderson Riots," also nationalistic in origin, occurred during the 1831-32 season at the Bowery Theater in New York. The attack on the theater is recorded in Philip Hone's diary:

> The house filled very early to suffocation. When I went in the whole interior was a solid mass of men. Not a single female present, except two or three in the upper tier. . . . Simpson came forward, attempted to read his apology. This was the signal for the commencement of the riot, and from that time the disturbance continued during the whole night. Apples, eggs, and other missiles were showered from the stage. . . . The street in front of the theatre was filled by the mob, the lamps were broken, and the interior sustained considerable injury.[104]

Hone's diary is also the source of information about another Bowery Theater riot on July 10, 1834: "An hour after the performance commenced, the mob broke open the doors, took possession of every part of the house, committed every species of outrage, hissed and pelted poor Hamblin, not regarding the talisman which he relied upon, the American flag, which he waved over his head."[105]

The Park Theater, New York's most elegant, was the scene of some unpleasant violence in May of 1836 upon the appearance of Mr. and Mrs. Joseph Wood. As the hissing and booing reached a high pitch, a copper coin struck Mrs. Wood on the face and, as Alston Brown described it, "a piece of a bench, six feet long, was thrown from the second tier, which Wood fortunately caught."[106]

In 1848 the Bowery had another riot caused by a rivalry between two actress-dancers. The audience smashed the theater's furnishings until the police arrived to clear the building "in order to save it from being a complete wreck."[107]

The most infamous example of theatrical violence in America occurred in 1849 in and around the Astor Place Opera House. This riot brought out the cavalry, the first divisions of the state militia, and the National Guard, who were attacked by the mob with paving stones as they attempted to reach the theater. Finally, cannons were posted outside the theater and, under a shower of bricks, paving stones and other heavy missiles, orders were issued to fire on the mob. By the end of the riot, twenty-one people had been killed, thirty-one wounded, and many others arrested.[108]

As one might expect, the theater of the frontier was, as Constance Rourke wrote, "a special arena for violence."[109] In the mining-town theaters of the West, often outgrowths of saloons, "duels were frequent and murder was common."[110] The diary of H. Watkins also records brawls and shoot-outs in Houston theaters between the militia and the gamblers who monopolized the front seats of the theaters in the 1840s.[111]

Even should the excesses of rowdiness and violence be remedied, the very basic activity of viewing a play, it was argued, was detrimental to the virtuous life fostered by the home because one surrendered judgment to illusion and emotion in viewing a play.[112] Even a moral play appealed overwhelmingly to emotion, passion, the senses, and the imagination: "Theatrical amusements have a direct tendency to awaken and strengthen those passions of our nature which it is at once our interest and our duty to curb and discipline."[113] The excitement, the overflow of any feeling, even a good one, was somehow unhealthy in itself. Detractors of the stage illustrated this by pointing out that Lord Byron had been so excited while watching Edmund Kean's portrayal in *Sir Giles Overreach* that he had gone into convulsions. It was also reported that numerous ladies on different occasions had fainted or had fits while watching plays.[114] The arguments against the theater on the grounds that it excites the faculties that should remain composed were summarized by the Reverend Samuel Winchester: "The tendency of theatrical amusement is to produce injurious excitement. The passions are inflamed, the sympathies are excited, and a multitude of various emotions crowd upon and often overwhelm the soul."[115] So while the ideal home was supposedly working to keep sensuality, emotion, and imagination in check, the theater was thriving on these very excesses, and, in the process, undermining the foundation of the family.

If the actress's professional world were the antithesis of the domestic ideal, she herself was the antithesis of ideal womanhood, that center

Violence: The Astor Place riot. (Harvard Theatre Collection)

of the American home, revered by the majority of the middle and upper classes in particular. The century identified the ideal woman as one who fulfilled the role to which nature and scripture had assigned her. Her "normal" position was "the charge of the household, and especially her calling as wife and mother."[116] Nature, it was believed, had dictated that she remain fairly close to her home, within "the inner circle,"[117] a trait noted by such travelers to America as Harriet Martineau and Alexis de Tocqueville.[118] Even within the home she modestly kept her place and did not intrude her opinion in matters of business and politics because she recognized her own limited reason and resolution, her own incompetence in logic and higher mathematics, her own poverty of leadership qualities.[119] As a result, the ideal woman left decisions regarding "religion, politics, business, social position and expenditure" to her husband. "She allows him to decide all these things. . . . It is a man's prerogative."[120] She was valued not for her strengths but for her weakness and was expected to remain in ignorance of financial matters. "Few of them were permitted any control over family finances," a situation which in reality often worked to the detriment of household efficiency.[121] As a result, the ideal American woman was something like Ibsen's Nora—a doll living in a doll's house.

Older, colonial values of industry and usefulness seem to have been exchanged for "ornamental idleness"[122]—social graces and feminine delicacy. The ideal woman was expected, according to Margaret Fuller, to prepare herself for a life of keeping house and sewing, "partly in the social circle, where her manners may be formed, ornamental accomplishments perfected and displayed."[123] Listed as one of her primary duties by Dr. L. P. Brockett is "the necessary time occupied in planning for her own wardrobe and that of her family, and the claims of society."[124] J. C. Furnas describes the ideal woman as reading sentimental novels, supervising servants who did most of the work, "dressing one way and then another to suit the clock," visiting other equally idle women, and occasionally painting, drawing, singing, or playing the piano.[125]

One of the few useful, as opposed to ornamental, roles assigned the ideal woman was her devotion to religious and moral duties, because she was the backbone of the religious congregation, and the church was the center of her social life.[126] To English and European travelers, the fervor and single-mindedness with which women were expected to, and did, turn to religion and clergymen was an extraordinary matter deserving special attention. Mrs. Trollope found that women crowded the churches from east to west. "Surely," she wrote, "there is no country in the world where religion makes so large a part of the amusement and occupation of the ladies. Spain, in its most Catholic days, could not exceed it."[127] Not only did hundreds of women crowd into individual Sunday morning church services and revivals, but they spent a great deal of the rest of their time at religious meetings. In Washington, Presbyterian women went to church three times on Sunday, and on the edge of the frontier "no evenings in the week but brings throngs of the young and beautiful to the chapels and meetinghouses."[128] J. S. Buckingham also referred to "the frequency of religious meetings, almost every evening of the week, engaging all the leisure of the women."[129] Mrs. Trollope was convinced that the relationship between women and the clergy had reached the point of being downright unhealthy:

> The influence which the ministers of all the innumerable religious sects throughout America, have on the females of their respective congregations, approaches very nearly to what we read of in Spain, or in other strictly Roman Catholic countries. There are many causes for this peculiar influence. Where equality of rank is affectedly acknowledged by the rich, and clamorously claimed by the poor, distinction and preeminence are allowed to the clergy only. This gives them high importance in the eyes of the ladies. I think, also, that it is from the clergy only that the women of America receive that sort of attention which is so dearly valued by every female heart throughout the world. With the priests of America, the women hold that degree of influential importance which, in the countries of Europe, is allowed them throughout all orders and ranks of society, except, perhaps, the very lowest; and in return for this they seem to give their hearts and souls into their keeping.[130]

In their zealous support of the church and churchmen, the women of America were consistent with idealized womanhood and its insistence that women be religious, to control their own base natures and to receive the training to fulfill their roles as moral teachers of children.

No portrait of the ideal American woman would be complete without mention of the attributes most crucial to her nature—purity, bordering on sainthood, and modesty. Margaret Fuller, in describing society's view of women, wrote: "She represents purity, and all that appertains to her should be kept delicately pure. She is modesty, and draperies should soften all rude lineaments, and exclude glare and dust."[131]

Her modesty kept her fairly aloof from encounters with men other than her husband or minister. Even in social situations to which both men and women were invited, Mrs. Trollope observed, the custom of having ladies retire to drawing rooms, separate from gentlemen, was much more strictly adhered to in America than it was in England and Europe.[132]

Modesty also meant that the ideal woman kept a fairly low profile. Anna Cora Mowatt had been harshly criticized by the press in 1842 for appearing publicly before men and women. Her biographer, Eric Barnes, noted that "it was bad enough that Mrs. Mowatt should read poetry in public, but that she should do so before mixed audiences seemed nothing less than depravity."[133] Mary Lyon, founder of Mount Holyoke College, is another of many examples of a woman who was strongly advised to cease her appearances before "mixed meetings."[134] Instances such as these led actress Olive Logan to ask, "Why, whenever a woman speaks about something, is there such a general feeling that something indelicate has been done?"[135] Even in the performance of her religious duties, the ideal woman was not to draw attention to herself by stepping out of her rightful place to speak in public. As a

Immodesty:
Dressing an actress'
hair. (John J.
Jennings, *Theatrical
and Circus Life*)

An orgy in the wine-room. (John J. Jennings, *Theatrical and Circus Life*)

result, when women sought church platforms in their work for abolition and temperance, causes that many of the clergy supported, they were frequently turned away because of the prohibition against women "exposing" themselves in public by speaking before mixed audiences. The extremity to which this could be carried was recorded by Matilda Gage, a nineteenth-century suffragette: "In 1843, the Hopkinson Association of Congregational Divines of New Hampshire unanimously enacted a statute in opposition to women opening their lips in church, even to 'sigh' or 'groan' in contrition."[136]

The actress, of necessity, deviated sharply from this nineteenth-century idealization of womanly purity, modesty, religiousness, and weakness, as of course did many other women of the age. By working outside the home, she had abandoned her "place," defined by nature and Holy Writ. When she supported male members of her family, she assumed an unnatural role and sought to overturn the biblically sanctioned social order in which woman is subservient to man. Actress-managers, in particular, lost that frailty and delicacy that were among woman's treasured attributes in soiling themselves with money matters.

Worse than these things, the actress, it was thought, had little claim on modesty. Her work required her to be in close association with men: she had to change costumes frequently in the same general backstage area with men; she often had to travel with men when shows went on tour; and on stage she would play love scenes with men. Untenably immodest behaviour was demanded of the actress on stage. She was seen dispensing "lascivious smiles, wanton glances, and dubious compliments."[137] She assumed "indelicate attitudes," kissed men on stage and engaged in "a variety of vain and sinful practices," undoubtedly betrayed by "heaving bosoms, languishing glances, voluptuous attitudes, falling into the arms of men,"[138] and allowing herself to be scantily attired and "twirled and handled on stage."[139]

The actress's most egregious deviation from ideal womanhood, in the eyes of the religious public, was her "impurity"—that is, immorality. Of this the public was absolutely sure. Olive Logan, herself a nineteenth-century actress and writer, deplored the fact that "the name of the poor stock actress is a synonym for what is lax in the sex."[140] This cruel misconception that equated most actresses with prostitutes, or "what is lax in the sex," arose in large measure because of the conditions on the Restoration stage—conditions to which critics alluded rather frequently. John Harold Wilson, in *All the King's Ladies,* recounted the genesis of a reputation, developed during the Restoration, that plagued actresses for two hundred years thereafter.[141] From the time when actresses were introduced to the English stage, around 1660, until the eighteenth century, the theater was a means by which actresses could become wives but more often mistresses of wealthy men. Of the eighty women who are known to have been actresses in London between 1660 and 1689, at least twelve, according to Wilson's research, left the stage to become mistresses or prostitutes. Twelve others who stayed on the stage had reputations as harlots. Of the eighty, probably no more than twenty-four led respectable lives. As a result, he wrote, "'actress' and 'whore' were effectively synonymous."[142] It was the reputation established at this time that clung to members of the profession in the nineteenth century in America, long after it had ceased to be accurate and had instead become a slander.

It was impossible to maintain that all actresses were bad women, but the historical antagonism between the stage and the church and the frequent divorces among actresses cast suspicion on them as a class: "to assume—what can be proved—that there is no sympathy, and never has been any, between members of this profession and evangelical piety

Drunkenness: Sobering a comedian. (John J. Jennings, *Theatrical and Circus Life*)

[because] domestic relations of actors and actresses have, in very many instances, exhibited the freedom which they so often illustrate on the stage."[143]

In the minds of many clergymen and churchgoers, a women's mere association with the stage made her immoral. No woman could remain on the stage and keep the purity of a saintlike femininity:

The effects of the kind of life led by players is peculiarly pernicious to female character. It strips it of all its loftier attributes, its softer and more

Working a "Greeny" at a matinee. (John J. Jennings, *Theatrical and Circus Life*)

delicate charms. Sensibility, modesty and refinement are gradually extin-
guished by the unfeminine and indelicate business of the stage, and nothing
is left but the hackneyed and haggard form of injured humanity, covered
and bedecked perhaps, by false and tawdry ornaments. A few female actors
may have preserved their virtue, but, alas! How many have lost it forever
by their connection with the stage. And if others have not been entirely
ruined by this means, how greatly must their characters have suffered in
purity and elevations, by the dark forms of evil with which they come into
such close and continual contact![144]

One confirmation of the public disapproval of actresses is the extent
to which members of the theatrical profession energetically and defen-
sively countered clerical arguments. While it must be admitted in
judging the soundness of these accounts that the authors—actors, managers, and stage historians of the time—had a certain vested interest
in upholding a profession that was usually under severe attack, their
reports have infinitely more validity than those of antagonistic clergy-

men and journalists who often boasted that they had never been inside a theater. The men of the American theater insisted, not only that actresses were more humanitarian than other women, but that even in terms of a very narrowly defined morality actresses were as respectable as other women. W. W. Clapp, a historian of the Boston stage, claimed that there was "no class in the community more remarkable for constancy and devotion in their domestic relations" than were actresses.[145] Another actor, William Davidge, defended actresses in a book entitled *The Drama Defended* by writing that "there are now in the city of New York, who have returned from the duties of their profession, those whose chastity, truthfulness, and domestic accomplishments, as daughters, wives and mothers, are second to none, not even the most opulent in this vast metropolis."[146] When actresses and ballet girls did become immoral, he continued, it was not the fault of the theater: "A young woman seldom falls or loses her self-respect because entrusted to her own guidance behind the scenes of a Theater; it is from without that the spoiler comes. It is very rarely from the profession, but from the followers of inexperience."[147] Nor, wrote Davidge, was there any truth in the argument that actresses are just naturally sinful because they work in close association with men: men and women worked together in factories and churches without being corrupted or compromised. Furthermore, he said, what seemed to be true onstage was not necessarily true offstage, as many ignorant critics of actresses thought: an actress who was affectionate toward an actor onstage might dislike him intensely in real life and scarcely be on speaking terms with him after the curtain fell.[148]

Theatrical women were particularly quick to rise in defense of their sister actresses, including the lowly ballet girls who were so often the prey of stage-door johnnies or "mashers." Anna Cora Mowatt, a latecomer to the stage, who had been suspicious of actors in her youth and felt insulted when a manager first offered her a stage position, came to the defense of actresses after she had acquired some firsthand knowledge of the profession. She indicated just how very wrong she had been in her self-righteous disdain. To her surprise, she had found "refined and accomplished ladies, exemplary wives" in the theater, and said, "My views concerning the stage and my estimate of the members of dramatic companies had undergone a total revolution. Many circumstances had proved to me how unfounded were the prejudices of the world against the profession as a body." Women in the theater, she found, led lives of "unimpeachable purity, industry, devotion to their kind, and fulfilling the hardest duties of life with a species of stoical heroism."[149]

Clara Morris's observations as an adult actress belied everything her mother had assumed about the theater. Morris claimed that, in all her years in the theater, she had seen only one instance of even a breath of scandal in the theaters where she had been employed.[150]

Despite these defenses, much of the church-going public persisted in the view that the actress was immoral and immodest. She was also regarded as falling far short of ideal womanhood in being removed from, even antagonistic to, religion. Other women crowded the churches as the centers of their social activities, but, contended Clara Morris, the "exclusive spirit" of churches kept actresses away. In an age when the minister was the idol of the ideal woman, he was the adversary of the actress. Morris was convinced that the public falsely assumed that individual actresses were even incapable of being religious at all and, as a class, were regarded as the enemies rather than the champions of religion.[151] Because of this, the actress seemed to bear a heavier burden than did other working women in her deviation from the ideal: she was regarded, not simply as failing to live up to the ideal, but as being symbolic of all that the ideal was not.

The outstanding stars of the American stage studied in this volume rarely if ever recorded social snubs or instances of slander in the press or from the pulpit. Very infrequently was there any complaint about their inability to move comfortably in polite society. We have only random hints of the reaction of the religious mainstream to these women, most of whom kept within the protective circle of the theatrical world. We do see, however, the circumstances of Mary Ann Duff's declining years when, in embracing the church, she had to dissociate herself from actors. We see her own and her family's attempt to hide her past as an actress.[152] We read of Fanny Kemble's discovering the strong objections to the theater in America and being unable to entertain old friends because her husband would not allow actors in his house.[153] One finds that Ann Cora Mowatt was brainwashed against the theater by her minister, then later was accused of betraying her class when she decided to become an actress, and finally, after her remarriage, suffered the snubs of Richmond society, not only because she was a Swedenborgian, but because she had been an actress.[154] One discovers that at the time of Lincoln's death, while Laura Keene attempted to calm a wild audience, some of the spectators were yelling, "Burn the theater!" and "Kill the actors!"[155] Such accounts in the life stories of these women are relatively few, but the climate of opinion reflected in these and other stories and sermons already cited was undeniably hostile toward the actress and her profession. As a class they were frequently excoriated by the public. So, whether or not actresses themselves or their biographers belabored the point, these women were living in an age that often regarded them and their profession as, at worst, dangerous and despicable and, at best, suspicious and peculiar—a truth of which they were abundantly aware.

Even though the religious public's opinion of actresses was distorted and exaggerated, it was, nevertheless, a strong and widely held opinion that cannot easily be dismissed. It is only with recognition of that opinion that one can detect an element of loneliness in the life of the actress who realized how far outside the mainstream of nineteenth-century womanhood she was. It is only with that recognition that one can imagine the actress's defensiveness, arising from constant attacks on her personal character. It is only with that recognition that one can understand the courage of the actress and the irony of her professional situation—at the same time the worst and the best of worlds.

Obviously, even the successful American actress in the nineteenth century was radically different from that day's view of what a woman should or could be. Her life was a constant repudiation of the inevitability of female limitation preached in America. Quite clearly, the theater provided actresses with a subculture wherein the psychological restrictions of the larger society were loosened. And that larger society, in its single-minded and largely wrongheaded fashion, interpreted and feared the deviations from "woman's proper sphere" solely as sexual looseness, even though the nonconformity of most actresses could best be described in economic and domestic terms rather than sexual ones.

# CHAPTER 2

# ENTER THE BREADWINNER

Because of the religious objections to the theater in the nineteenth century, an actress was pulled in antipodal directions, for at the same time that she was excoriated, she was afforded in the theater one of the very few opportunities not only to earn independence and a living wage but also, ironically, to gain a measure of self-respect. Above all, this disparaged profession gave her, if she were ambitious and talented, the possibility of economic and professional equality with men which she could find nowhere else.

The nation as a whole was experiencing vast commercial awakenings and enlargements, but the vocational growth of its women in most professions was stunted by greater psychological, social, and economic restrictions which somehow placed them outside of life's mainstream and forbade them to compete with men for wages and for positions of professional prominence. Only within that larger context of women and work in the nineteenth century can one appreciate the opportunity in the theater to circumvent many of the restrictions placed on most women.

The young girl approaching womanhood and the prospect of a vocation in the early nineteenth century stepped into an economic current which had taken its course in the last decades of the eighteenth century. Her mother and grandmother had lived in a sparsely populated, rural America where essential industries—the weaving of cloth, the sewing of garments,

The sweat-shop system required its workers to sew in factories all day and then carry home heavy burdens to work on all night. (*Harper's Weekly*, April 26, 1890)

the making of shoes and hats—were carried on largely by families under their own roofs. It was a society in which women as well as men engaged in the full range of necessary occupations. There would have been women in those colonial communities of her mother's and grand-mother's day who owned and managed their own shops, others who read and practiced law, medicine, and trades, side by side with their husbands. Both her mother and grandmother, in both North and South, would have expected their children to be delivered by a woman, for with few exceptions, obstetrics was the sole province of women.[1] As Daniel Boorstin wrote in *The Americans*, "women in the colonies were successful in more different activities and were more prominent in professional and public life than they would be again until the twentieth century."[2] Whether or not the young nineteenth-century woman re-alized it, her mother and her mother's mother had enjoyed, not only greater professional opportunities, but probably greater personal free-dom than she herself would know, restricted as she was by a more rigid moral code and an increasingly secure double standard that was unapologetically applied to virtually every sphere of human life— business, politics, religion, social behavior, and sex.[3] Above all, the emerging nineteenth-century woman was hampered by the stricter interpretation of "woman's place."

She stepped into the current of industrialization that had already gathered momentum with the cotton mills that rose in the pastoral eighteenth-century countryside of the Northeast, with the power loom developed at the turn of the century and the assembly-line process begun with Eli Whitney's dramatic demonstration of the manufacture of rifles, and that would continue in later inventions crucial to her vocational life. Elias Howe's sewing machine introduced in 1846 and the typewriter in 1873 are just two examples. The young nineteenth-century woman would also, no doubt, be aware of the fruits of that revolution—some of them exceedingly bitter. Already by 1800, a greater proportion of women than ever before was working outside the home, many in the newly established mills of the Northeast. Already the numbers of people in the nation were growing at a phenomenal rate—a country of over 3 million in 1790 would reach 23 million by 1850. Already by 1800, population, shops, and services were beginning to be drawn into the cities.[4]

As the emerging culture crystalized, virtually no women would be directly involved in the high finance and politics of the nineteenth-century man's world—the world of land speculation, rapid capital investment in industry and transportation, and easy credit. But each woman, nevertheless, would be marked—some only slightly, others profoundly—by the results that characterized the whole century: periods of flush times and spiraling costs alternating with depressions, panics, and chronic unemployment.[5]

If the rapid growth of technology and industry had attracted a young woman to the city in the boom produced by the War of 1812, she might well have found herself unemployed in the depression that followed in 1817. If she were still unmarried, she probably noted the first wave of young men leaving her and their own financial hopelessness behind for the promise of work in the West. During the first half of the century, young men in increasing numbers were lured westward by land, by gold, and by adventure, to escape the cycles of further depressions and poverty. The five-year panic beginning in 1837 closed factories and left one-third of New York City out of work. Young men left behind larger and larger numbers of unmarried girls who had to support themselves in lieu of marriage, in spite of the bad times, and who, ironically, were increasingly needed by industry because of the male exodus.

Whether a girl grew up in the first or the last of the century, one constant paradoxical trap remained, an impossibly complex situation that placed her between Scylla and Charybdis: while economic changes lured her, even forced her, out of the home to work, more often than not, middle- and upper-class attitudes placed a moral stigma on her for venturing out of the sphere of her own home. Inventions and the growth of machinery were robbing her of the traditional homebound work, while Holy Writ, capitalistic custom, and her very nature, as the century viewed it, dictated that she was created to stay at home and grace it with the performance of special, limited duties. After 1800, the idea of "woman's place," which has already been discussed in the context of the century's religious climate, grew increasingly strong, increasingly rigid and idealized.[6] Women writers of very different persuasions acknowledged the idea of woman's place and woman's duty as their age dictated it. A nineteenth-century woman named Eliza Farrar wrote in her book of advice, *The Young Lady's Friend,* that whether a woman were rich or poor, housework was "her express vocation," "her peculiar calling."[7] Margaret Fuller also recognized the century's definition of woman's place: "Much has been written about woman's keeping within her sphere, which is defined as the domestic sphere. As a little girl she is to learn the lighter family duties, while she acquires that limited acquaintance with the realm of literature or science that will enable her to superintend the instruction of children."[8]

Religion, nature, and capitalism, as the age interpreted each, dictated her place. The Bible told her to be subservient to man. A typical argument, using biblical support, was offered by a nineteenth-century physician, Dr. L. P. Brockett:

> We can infer that it was not the intention of the Almighty to create as a help-meet for Adam one who should be in all respects his peer or equal. . . . This very language of both Adam and the Creator implies, in some degree, a subordination to the man, whose helper she is to be. With the Divine approval, Adam assumes the right to assign to her a name, as he had previously done to the animal creation. . . . We have already noticed how this authority of the man, with subordination of the woman, is still more distinctly stated in the sentence pronounced upon the woman, after her temptation and fall, and in part, we must believe, because she had undertaken to act independently of her associate and head.[9]

Because woman was believed to be subservient to man, she was advised not to leave her sphere to compete with him or to supervise him. Her foremost jobs were to be the supporter of her husband and the moral teacher of his children.

Nature itself had made her unfit for most work outside the home. She was naturally weak in her ability to reason, to generalize, to connect ideas, to judge, and to persevere.[10] Brockett noted that "woman has but little genius for invention; she may apply or adapt an invention to some purpose for which it was not at first intended, though she does this but rarely." He was also convinced that "this lack of creative power manifests itself also in her writings."[11] Alexander Walker, another nineteenth-century student of female psychology, was even more blunt in describing woman's natural limitations: "Her friendship, her philanthropy, her patriotism and her politics, requiring the exercise of reason, are so feeble as to be worthless."[12]

The dictates of capitalism, added to special readings of the Bible and singular beliefs about woman's nature, also served to inhibit woman's options as a worker. The new capitalist proved his success by his accumulation of material goods, which included a wife who could be maintained in "ornamental idleness."[13] In short, the ideal woman was an object meant to grace the home of the successful businessman. As Mari Jo Buhle, Ann D. Gordon, and Nancy E. Schrom wrote in their history of working women in America, "The older traditions of feminine usefulness, strength and duty were cast aside for moral and decorative functions."[14] This attitude led to a lack of respect for women who did any kind of work.[15] Margaret Fuller, writing from the vantage point of the time, observed the value that her age placed on woman's ornamental idleness, even as the young girl was prepared for marriage: "It is not generally proposed that she should be sufficiently instructed and developed to understand the pursuits or aims of her future husband; she is not to be a help-meet to him in the way of companionship and counsel, except in the care of his house and children."[16] The prevailing judgment, deplored by Fuller, persisted to the end of the century, one critic declaring, "It is unbecoming for her to enter any of the professions, she is not fitted for toil; she was never meant for a breadwinner; her place is the home."[17] The result of these and other forces rendered her, ideally, helpless in the world of work, helpless in financial matters, worthless in politics. Consequently, the woman at home, idle, with the possible exception of a role as moral teacher, was the ideal, and insofar as choice or necessity moved her to deviate from it, she trod dangerous ground, teetering on the edge of moral disaster, if not actually becoming tainted by the mere displacement.

The problem, of course, was that she did not always have the chance to be a middle-class, nineteenth-century fireside angel. She did not always have a home to stay in, much less a choice. Even the staunchest guardians of woman's rightful place had to acknowledge that untoward circumstances often threw women out of their own domestic circle to find work: widowhood; desertion; divorce; spinsterhood; a husband's illness, irresponsibility or ill fortune—all were very real catastrophies and were ineluctably beyond a woman's control. What then could she do when, for whatever reason, she was thrown into the work force? The notion that women were by nature severely limited—not just physically but intellectually and emotionally as well—worked to curtail the options acceptable to a straitlaced society as surely as did legal restrictions.

For educated and uneducated women alike, the options were equally meager, often dismal. Despite the force of economic necessity, delicacy dictated that a woman consider first those occupations that could be conducted within her house—if she had one: she could take in washing or sewing or do piecework. If these chores were not to her liking, she might consider keeping bees or, as Dr. Brockett advised, cultivating and gathering "small fruits."[18]

The plain truth is that many women had no choice but to sacrifice delicacy in order to eke out the most elemental survival. The possibilities were few, and the work available was typically demeaning, debilitating, and hopeless. When she did not have the means to "cultivate small fruits," the woman seeking to earn her own livelihood turned to the new urbanized, industrialized society, and here, strangely enough, even began to dominate certain types of employment. Woman was the mainstay of the cotton mill and of the silk and the lace factory and was, in addition, being employed in increasing numbers in shoe, wool, and hat factories.[19] Of course, she also continued to sew the clothes for a nation and to do domestic chores for other, more fortunate women. During the last half of the century, a limited group of women, most of them native born, gradually moved upwards to such white-collar jobs as telegraph operator, typist, and government clerk.

To look at the mere numbers of jobs available for uneducated women, however, without recognizing the conditions under which they worked is to have an incomplete and distorted picture. From the vantage point of the worker, that picture was almost universally harsh. Even the famous textile mills of Lowell, Massachusetts, built in 1823 to meliorate the gross abuses of the industrial revolution and shown to European visitors as model establishments, were themselves heavily paternalistic and restricting in their best days; nor were they immune from deteriorating working conditions as the century wore on.[20] Conditions in most factories, moreover, were distinctly less than model and, in many instances, hardly humane.

In 1817 a day in the cotton mills of Fall River, Massachusetts, began around five in the morning and lasted until seven-thirty at night. One-half hour was allowed the girls at midday to rush home, eat, and return to work; and when they finished in the evening they were usually too weary to eat at all.[21] Everywhere the cotton mills were generally unventilated and filled with cotton dust and the fumes from oil lamps. If a girl or woman were lucky, she could perhaps go into domestic service, generally considered a step upward over factory work. But here, too, the situation was far from ideal. Servants were on call twenty-four hours a day, seven days a week.[22] The more highly regarded trades of white-collar worker and salesgirl were scarcely better. Saleswomen had to stand behind their counters throughout the long day, 5:00 A.M. until 10:00 P.M. for six days a week, and half day on Sunday, when inventory was taken. Like factory workers, they were fined for tardiness or for overstaying their alloted three to five minutes in the company bathrooms.[23] Even at the close of the century, when industrial barons enjoyed unparalleled luxury, the conditions of their workers were still abominable. Helen Campbell's report of the 1893 findings of the Massachusetts Bureau of Labor is hair-raising:

The low-paid, restricted life of a teacher was open to the educated woman. (L. P. Brockett, *Woman: Her Rights, Wrongs, Privileges, and Responsibilities*)

Some were in . . . basements where dampness was added to cold and bad air. . . . In one case girls were working in "little pens all shelved over. . . . There are no conveniences for women; and men and women use the same closets, wash basins, and drinking cups, etc." . . . In another a water-closet in the center of the room filled it with a sickening stench. . . . Feather-sorters, fur-workers, cotton-sorters, all workers on any material that gives off dust, are subject to lung and bronchial troubles. In soap factories the girls' hands are eaten by the caustic soda, and by the end of the day the fingers are often raw and bleeding. In making buttons, pins and other manufactures . . . there is always liability of getting the fingers jammed or caught. For the first three times the wounds are dressed without charge. After that the person injured must pay expenses. . . .

In food preparation girls who clean and pack fish get blistered hands and fingers from saltpetre. . . . Others in "working stalls" stand in cold water all day. . . .

In match-factories . . . necrosis often attacks the worker, and the jaw is eaten away. . . .[24]

Campbell's report, as well as other accounts of women's work, indicates that, while the century needed women's labor, employers were scarcely willing to share the benefits of industrialism with them.

The cultivated, educated woman was no more immune from the exigencies of death and fortune and the harsh economic limitations imposed on women than was the potential factory or domestic worker. In another time, with the proper desire and ability, she might have entered one of the professions; but the girl who determined to enter any major profession except teaching in the first half of the century could only be described as a hopeless dreamer. Law, medicine, even business were virtually closed to her. There were only a handful of women lawyers in the entire country in the 1880s and 1890s,[25] and the cohort of women shopkeepers, fairly numerous in the eighteenth century, had dwindled sharply by 1830. Even careers auxiliary to business became less available. An anonymous contributor of an article on women and work in the 1860s protested that "the very idea of a woman wanting to keep books was ridiculed as something beyond belief."[26] Those nineteenth-century women who did manage careers as doctors or lawyers or businesswomen are the exceptions whose names are held up in history books as being phenomenal, not typical of the time.

Women were frozen out of professions not only by changing economic forces and shifting conceptions of the ideal woman but also by developments in professional training. Contrary to colonial practice, professionals in the nineteenth century had to be trained formally, often in universities, and they had to be certified to practice. But neither the requisite training nor admission to the university nor the certification was easily forthcoming for women. None of the education that a young woman might muster beyond the secondary level was likely to prepare her for the hard task of self-support. She might, at her family's pleasure, attend secondary school, but it was best that she not entertain any illusions about emerging with a liberal education, much less any professional skill. The curricula were notoriously trivial and impractical for all but the would-be doll-like wives of comfortably situated husbands. Such women would learn to do needle work, paint, play a musical instrument, sing, and perhaps draw. They would be well equipped to arrange flowers and serve tea to other women in their drawing rooms.

Only in 1837 did the first women's institution of higher learning open—Mount Holyoke Seminary in South Hadley, Massachusetts. And despite the crying need for education and the immense energy of those in the fore of the movement to provide women with education, the first college degree was not awarded a woman until 1841. Even as late

If all else failed, a woman could always cultivate small fruits. (L. P. Brockett, *Woman: Her Rights, Wrongs, Privileges, and Responsibilities*)

as the Civil War, the number of women with college degrees was small. Throughout the century, the only profession that continued to be deemed suitable for women, despite the limited education afforded them, was teaching. In sum, their occupational plight was very real because of the prejudices of the age, as Dr. L. P. Brockett acknowledged:

> She may teach a small school at home, or perhaps take a position as assistant teacher in some public school, or she may teach music or drawing, or French or German, if she can obtain pupils, or manage a small store. This comprises about the entire list of occupations which are within her reach, and all are precarious and often inadequate for her purpose.[27]

Finally, as unlike as the educated and uneducated women might be in background and capabilities, when misfortune forced them into the job market, they faced a common future of discouragement, limitation, and injustice. Whether conditions of a woman's job were pleasant or hard, whether she were skilled or not, she could depend in the typical position on one fundamental reality, so widespread and longstanding as scarcely to be noted: she would inevitably receive far less money than would men for the same kind and quality of work. She also faced another constant and disheartening reality, whether she worked outside the home or not and whether she were educated or not: that reality was servitude. The woman teacher, like the domestic worker, was inevitably under someone else's supervision. It was the rare situation, almost freakish, to find a woman in a position of financial or political leadership or to find one working with any degree of independence.

In such a world where the shop girl was broken, the factory worker was tied with the iron chains of poverty to the machines that could kill her, where even the cultivated woman, cast out on her own, often felt the cold threat of nonexistence close in around her, in such a world designed to atrophy the courage and imagination of the hardiest women, one field stood apart as a viable aspiration for both educated and uneducated women of talent and ambition. That possibility was the stage. For the women who entered its portals, opportunities for financial reward, professional status, and even a surprising measure of equality with men were within reach as they were almost nowhere else.

The history of the theater's development in the nineteenth century suggests that a young woman who chose a career in the theater allied herself with a rapidly growing, vital profession. The developing industrialization, the growth of cities, the expansion across the plains, the sudden opening up of the West, especially California—all worked to facilitate its spread. By the turn of the nineteenth century, the American theater was young but healthy. Boston, New York, Philadelphia, Baltimore, Charleston, Richmond, Norfolk, Washington, and other cities already possessed buildings for theater. New York's Park Theater held as many as two thousand patrons. Several cities offered a full season of plays and had already attracted resident companies. The Chestnut Street Theater, built by subscription in 1794 by the citizens of Philadelphia, is one example.[28]

Nor was the theater entirely restricted to large urban areas, even in the first decade of the century. By 1800 three separate circuits were bringing theater to virtually all the smaller towns in the East: one, based in Charleston, toured Richmond and the Southeast; another, based in New York and Boston, covered smaller towns in the Northeast; and a third, operating from Philadelphia, toured as far south as Baltimore and Annapolis. By the 1830s several cities in the East even boasted more than one theater: New York had the Park, the Chatham, the Bowery, and the short-lived Lafayette; Philadelphia had the Walnut Street and the Chestnut Street; and Boston had the Federal Street and the Tremont.

Even during the first decades of the century, theater began moving westward into the Ohio Valley and toward the Mississippi River, eventually stretching across the plains to California. In 1815 a company put together by Samuel Drake, once a stage manager for the Albany Theater, traveled by wagon and flatboat and on foot toward Kentucky. Between 1815 and 1830, Drake firmly established theater in the Ohio Valley by developing a circuit to include the river towns of Kentucky and Ohio. Another pioneer, James H. Caldwell, staked his claim further south, arriving in New Orleans in 1819 to produce plays at both the English- and French-language theaters there and eventually, in 1824, to open a new establishment, the Camp Street Theater. During the next three years he toured as far north as St. Louis. He controlled theater in the entire Mississippi Valley for over ten years until Noah Ludlow and Sol Smith, who had already established their own circuits in Missouri, Tennessee, Alabama, and Louisiana, assumed Caldwell's territory as well.

The professional life of Noah Ludlow, an actor and manager of prominence in the first half of the nineteenth century, illustrates the extent to which theater covered even what was then considered rural frontier territory. Ludlow began his career by working with the Albany Theater in New York State in 1813. There he met Noble Luke Usher, a theatrical entrepreneur who claimed to have previously started three theaters in Kentucky. In 1815 Ludlow himself, in part inspired by Usher's stories of success, set out as a member of Samuel Drake's company, heading for Kentucky but stopping all along the way to perform in small towns—Cherry Valley, Cooperstown, Skeneateles, Canandaigua, and other communities farther south. Eventually he reached established theaters in Frankfort and Louisville. Beginning with this tour in 1815, during a lifetime as an actor and manager, Ludlow regularly brought theatricals to New Orleans, Mobile, Huntsville, Montgomery, Tuscaloosa, St. Louis, and Natchez. In 1853 he and his partner, Sol Smith, gave their farewell appearance.[29]

In 1833 Chicago had its first professional production and by 1847, its first theater building. Theaters arrived in the Far West in 1849, not long after the miners did. By 1852 Sacramento and San Francisco had several resident theaters which often presented full seasons. Even small mining camps had theatricals available to them, since actors, either independently or in companies, constantly toured these outposts, bringing theater to the goldfields even before permanent towns were established. There might even be, as Lotta Crabtree and her mother found out in the 1850s, two or three establishments in one small camp that regularly featured some kind of entertainment[30]—even though many of these theatrical facilities, in San Francisco as well as in out-of-the-way camps, were no more than saloons, gambling halls, and bawdy houses. From 1849 on, actors poured west to meet the high demand for entertainment and to cash in on comparatively good profits and opportunities there in the new city companies and in the mining camps. Constance Rourke's description of the theatrical scene, as Lotta Crabtree's mother might have seen it in the early 1850s, is worth quoting:

> San Francisco was full of actors. They had come from the show-boats of Mississippi, from the small theaters of Mobile, New Orleans, Galveston, Nashville, Cincinnati, from New York—actors, opera singers, musicians of all orders, vaudeville and circus performers, bands and bandmasters. They had converged from the ends of the earth. . . . They had come by steamer or small sailing craft around the Horn or even across the plains on foot. One company had traveled from St. Louis in prairie schooners with friendly Sioux as companions for part of the distance.[31]

With a bit less fanfare, perhaps, theater also moved into other frontiers along with the population: Houston had its first theatrical presentation in 1838, Galveston at least by 1839.[32] Utah built its famous Mormon Theater in 1861. The profession took a novel and expansive turn when the Chapmans popularized one of the first show-boats in 1830 and for ten years brought comedy, tragedy, melodrama, and music to settlements on the Mississippi River. From the thirties onward, actors performed on water as well as land, on boats designed primarily for theater and on ordinary riverboats equipped for theatrical presentations.[33]

In short, theater followed the frontier and the centers of population, becoming established along with the towns, providing amusement and a touch of civilization. The development in every area followed a somewhat similar pattern. A touring company would arrive in town to perform in the best available structure—a store, a hotel, a dining hall, a warehouse, a meeting hall, a saloon, or a house. Conditions were inevitably crude at first. Joseph Jefferson recorded an amusing example of primitive conditions in rural Illinois where his parents performed in scoured-out pigs' quarters.[34] Noah Ludlow told of a performance of his company in the second floor of a large, old house in Montgomery, Alabama.[35] Similar situations were found in the Far West. Constance Rourke reconstructed the rough settings in which Lotta Crabtree first performed in California:

They played in bar-rooms; and since many a bar was the village store, the troupe put on their entertainment in the midst of smoked ham and canned meats, red and blue flannel shirts strung across a line, and mining implements stacked by a counter. . . . Red calico was strung as curtains at the windows and draped over bunks built in the side-walls. A small stage would be contrived of saw-horses, or even by tying two billiard tables together, with woolen blankets hung in front for curtains.[36]

No matter how primitive the facilities might be, the company usually tolerated them as long as it could draw an audience. Cities that had some size and demand for drama would eventually build structures especially designed for productions, to accommodate touring shows. Finally, many large cities would be sufficiently interested in theater to support resident companies. Thereafter, theatrical tours would emanate from the city to outlying towns.

For the first half of the century, the resident stock company seemed to dominate theatrical activity in America. By 1860 there were more than fifty stock companies alone in this country.[37] In addition, of course, there were many other modes of theatrical entertainment besides the stock company: individual players and singers were booked into halls; temporarily organized troupes continued to tour, and hundreds of minstrel shows, both resident and touring, covered the country, although the latter did not at first employ actresses. The impressive variety and multiplicity achieved in theatrical activity by mid-century is suggested by the following partial list of establishments, mentioned by George C. D. Odell as offering entertainments in just one city— New York—in just one season—1851-52: the Broadway, Burton's, the Bowery, the National, Brougham's Lyceum, the Olympic, Niblo's, the Astor Place Opera House, Niblo's Garden, Tripler Hall, Barnum's Museum, Vauxhall Gardens, Castle Garden, Brooklyn Museum, Metropolitan Hall, Chinese Concert Hall, Bleecker Hall, Stuyvesant Institute, Cupid Lyceum, the Temple of the Graces, the Tabernacle, Eagle Hall Shakespeare Hotel, the National Concert Hall, Mager's Conzert Hall, Altenkirsch and Lang's, Coblenzer's Hotel, the Broadway Casino, the Warren Hotel, Charles Echart's Hotel, the National Hotel, Deutsches Vaudeville Theater, Bechtner's Hotel, a number of other German summer theaters in Manhattan and surrounding areas, the Liston Museum, the Gothic Hall, Fellow's Minstrel Hall, Wood's Minstrel Hall, White's Melodeon, the Franklin Museum, Knickerbocker Hall, Montague Hall and the Society Library.[38]

In 1860, the traveling show, given an immense boost by the development of the railroad, began to replace the old independent stock company. In the new kind of traveling shows, known as "combinations," the play itself was often the star. A company of actors would take one successful play on the road. Jack Poggi, in his study of theater and economics, found that, in the 1876-77 season, close to one hundred combinations toured the country. By 1904 that number had reached four hundred twenty.[39]

Thus, the sheer numbers of theaters and companies in the century, as well as the breadth and vitality of theatrical activity, is evidence that the theater could be a viable profession for many women in a time when the vocational choices were few and dismal. In the beginning of this burgeoning business, encouraged by the growth of cities and transportation, opportunities for women were relatively good. As theaters multiplied, so did the jobs for actresses. The stock company in William Dunlap's time, at the turn of the century, hired about eleven regular actresses as well as a number of supernumeraries, or "supers": the spearholders, the extras—members of crowds hired for a particular show to be at a certain spot at a certain time and to shout, stand, cheer, or just be there.[40] A good example of the acting jobs available as theater began to be established is the 1806 Philadelphia company that hired nine men and eleven women plus an undetermined number of supers,[41] and the New York company in 1798 that hired ten men and ten women. John Bernard, an actor who recorded the American scene in *Retrospections on America*, looked back with pleasure on the profession in the first quarter of the century: an actor in those early years was easily employable and, when not called upon to appear in a production, could augment his or her salary by doing readings in small towns.[42] By 1843 a typical stock company, like Wallacks or the Boston Museum, hired as many as twenty men and twenty women.[43] Touring companies used fewer women. Sol Smith apparently went on tour in 1833 with nine men and only four women, and he and Noah Ludlow usually toured with less than twenty women: seven in 1836, four in 1845, and thirteen in 1850.[44]

By the 1830s, when such professions as law, medicine, and business had been closed to women for some time, jobs in the theater were more accessible to women than they had ever been.[45] Statistics collected by Joseph A. Hill in *Women in Gainful Occupations, 1870-1920,* show that in 1870 there were more women in the theater than in medicine, including nursing; twenty times more actresses than newspaperwomen;

four times more women in the theater than in literary and scientific vocations combined; about one hundred forty times more actresses than women lawyers. The only profession that had more women than did the theater was teaching. In the 1880s, only teachers and nurses outnumbered actresses.[46]

Although the stage offered many women employment, few began their careers in good speaking roles. The actress would frequently start out by filling one of the humbler places in a company, as, for example, a supernumerary. Positions for women as well as men were defined by rather rigid lines of business. The basic female positions were a leading lady, a second lady, a juvenile lead, an old woman, a heavy, one or two singing chambermaids, a character actress, and several women known, in descending order of importance, as "walking ladies," "responsible utility actresses," and "utility ladies."[47] Most actresses began at the bottom as supernumararies or utility actresses. In the 1840s those with talent and initiative could move up in the cast after a three- or four-month apprenticeship. As time went on, it took longer and longer, sometimes even a year, for a super to become a utility actress. One avenue an actress could take to gain notice was to appear in the afterpieces, playlets given after the main attraction. Benefits also allowed the eager young actress to demonstrate her abilities. On those nights when established actors were given the opportunity to put together a performance from which they garnered most of the profit, apprentice actors were often requested to take longer roles than they normally were assigned. In any case, a novice who got beyond the supernumerary line had an excellent opportunity in a stock company to learn her craft by playing many different kinds of small roles, and if her performances were promising, earning promotion.

A development in the 1830s opened up many more jobs for women in the theater: the trend of introducing pageantry, musicals, and opera.[48] Eventually these productions led to the development of one of the largest groups of employees in the theater—the ballet corps, frequently mentioned by Anna Cora Mowatt, Olive Logan, and Clara Morris. Morris had actually begun her own career as a member of the ballet corps. In 1882, J. J. Jennings, a professional stage watcher, drew attention to a theater's call for fifty ballet girls for just one St. Louis production—a number he said was not unusual. They were drawn from the unemployed working force, the lower classes: "The majority of girls who answer for 'ladies for the ballet,'" Jennings wrote, "are shop girls, girls who take work to their homes, girls thrown out of employment, poor girls who had no other way of honestly earning a dollar."[49] Like supers, some ballet girls could expect eventual promotion to acting jobs, even stardom—Clara Morris is a shining example. She was, while a member of the ballet corps, given a small secondary speaking role, then assigned boys' parts, later given a chance to understudy more important roles, and finally, after proving her abilities, given a regular acting position in one of the "lines" of business.[50]

Naturally the stage did not guarantee instant stardom to every woman who presented herself at the door. Nor could every woman expect an immediate place in a theater company as an actress. But many women did find instant employment in the theater in various other capacities. As early as 1792, the stage was recommended as an answer for unemployed women by those who did not share the usual prejudices against the stage. It could be a means of preserving "the indigent helpless female from the necessity of earning bread by improper means."[51] Nineteenth-century actresses who wrote memoirs of the stage (Anna Cora Mowatt, writing in the 1830s and 1840s; Olive Logan, writing about the 1850s and 1860s; and Clara Morris, about the 1870s and 1880s) all agreed that the stage offered women one of the few self-respecting occupational alternatives. Morris stressed it as a realistic choice in a limited world that demanded servitude of its women:

> Some impetuous young reader who speaks first and thinks afterward may cry out that I am not doing justice to this profession of acting, even that I discredit it, in thus comparing it with humble and somewhat mechanical vocations; so before I go farther, little enthusiasts, let me remind you of the wording of this present query. It does not ask what advantage has acting over other professions, over other arts, but "What advantage has it over other occupations for women?"[52]

Although Olive Logan was more candid about the hardships of acting, a way of life to which she returned solely from necessity, she was as convinced as Morris that the living offered women by the theater was not to be taken lightly. The stage, beyond a doubt, gave women a rare opportunity to work in a society of many closed doors. Logan or Morris were not blind to the hardships and frustrations of acting, but they considered it to be one of the few respectable alternatives for women. In the light of all the hardships of the stage, wrote Logan, a man's desire to become an actor was not as understandable as a woman's desire to be an actress. In one of her stories, an experienced woman challenges an aspirant actor: "But, why do you desire to go upon the stage, Mr. Pennyweight? You cannot wish thus to earn a livelihood. If you were a woman—or even a poor man, I might understand it. The channels in which woman can work are few, and obstructed by numberless toilers."[53]

One reason why women were unable to enter so many other vocations was that they were often thrown into the work force so suddenly that they had neither the time nor the funds to acquire the training demanded by those open occupations that might be suitable otherwise. A woman could not even do the humble work of sewing or teaching painting and music without some training period. Meanwhile, no income could be realized until the skill was mastered. If she had the funds to wait, she might be able to train herself. But many could not wait. Logan dramatized the situation in the story of "Carrie Lee, an American Debutant":

> Being suddenly left fatherless, motherless and penniless, Carrie Lee was made painfully conscious of the fact that landladies, whatever their sympathies, do not keep boarders for nothing; and that the only irresistible music in this world is the jingle of a well-filled purse.
>
> Knowing then that she must do something for a livelihood, Carrie Lee investigated the subject of women's employment.
>
> But what could she do? Alas! here was the trouble. Carrie Lee had received a good boarding-school education, such as young ladies of the present day commonly receive—a smattering of French, a smattering of algebra, a smattering of drawing, a smattering of music and a smattering of various other genteel accomplishments—all of which were of very small use to her now. They would not, or so it seemed, bring her in five cents a day.
>
> In fact Carrie had never been taught anything useful in the world— there is not one girl in a thousand who ever *is* taught anything useful, or anything which she could turn to practical account if she were obliged to earn a livelihood.
>
> What *should* she do? Coloring photographs, dress-making, plain sewing, all these things require time and instruction before a livelihood can be made from them; and in the case of Carrie Lee the material wants were immediate, and must be immediately supplied.[54]

Of course, Logan, herself an actress, suggested the stage at mid-century as the solution to the problem of a girl such as Carrie. Not only could she be employed immediately, but she could also be paid as she learned. Clara Morris, writing of a later period, in the 1870s and 1880s, agreed: "The theater is, I think, the only place where a salary is paid to students during all the time they are learning their profession; surely a great, a wonderful advantage over other professions to be self-sustaining from the first."[55]

The stage not only provided many women with jobs; it also gave them fair wages—sometimes even extremely good wages—compared with other occupations. As Clara Morris was told by a young ballet girl when she first entered the theater, "everything in the theater's make-believe—except salary day."[56] A comparison of the standard wages paid to stock company actors, including ballet girls, with wages paid to female workers in other occupations in America gives the contemporary reader some idea of the economic life of theatrical women. It takes little imagination to see a very bleak life for working women in the salary figures for women throughout the century. For example, Matthew Carey, a philanthropist interested in the plight of seam-stresses, found that in 1831 the earnings of these women rarely exceeded $1.12 a week. At times they cleared only $.04 a day for food, fuel and clothing.[57] Barbara Wertheimer, in her study of working women, indicated that the wages for Lowell mill girls, "about the highest that women could command in the early part of the century," were $.35 to $.50 a day plus room and board.[58] She found further that in 1845 half the women workers in New York City earned less than $2.00 a week.[59] Dr. William Sanger, who made a study of prostitution in the city in 1858, found that female domestic servants, often on call twenty-four hours a day, made $5.00 a month or less. Seamstresses, tobacco packers, and book folders, many of whom eventually turned to pros-titution out of sheer weariness, averaged only a dollar a week.[60]

In the 1860s, thirty thousand female factory workers in New York City received an average salary of $.33 a day. At the same time, sewing machine operators earned from $5.00 to $8.00 a week, out of which they had to pay $3.00 or $4.00 for a "a bed in a wretched room, often with several other occupants, and without a window. . . ."[61] By 1868, another large group of women employees, milliners, were averaging from $4.00 to $7.00 a week, saleswomen from $6.00 to $7.00.[62] As late as 1893, the average salary for working women in New York City was still only $.60 a day, ranging from $2.00 a day for cashiers to $.30 a day for East Side factory workers, who, incidentally, worked from twelve to fifteen hours a day.[63]

Educated women who worked as teachers were also scarcely earning living wages. A Horace Mann report of 1847 indicates that the average pay per month for female teachers in the United States ranged from $4.75 in Vermont to $10.09 in Pennsylvania. It stands to reason that they also received board in addition to this wage.[64] A writer for the *Nation* in 1867 claimed that few women teachers ever got more than $600 yearly.[65]

Compared with these salaries, the wages of women in the theater appear to be very good indeed, especially when one considers the less grueling, less demeaning work in the theater.[66] While factory girls were making $.33 a day in the 1840s, supernumeraries, at the very bottom of the theatrical salary scale, were paid from $.25 to $.50 a night for relatively light work and few hours and, as has already been indicated, they might expect to move up to better roles and better salaries after several months if they were talented and interested.[67] The beginning salary at mid-century for a ballet girl was, it is true, only $3.00 or $4.00 a week, but even that was four times what skilled female labor was being paid by many employers. The ballet girl worked long and hard, but the work was not nearly so unpleasant or so hopeless and demeaning as domestic and factory work. Furthermore, the ballet girl could expect a raise to $8.00 a week within the month and, as she learned her trade, could move up to positions that paid even more. Theater people, at least, testified that even the poor wages of the ballet girl were much better than women could find in any other line of work.[68]

For those on the next step up the theatrical ladder, the ordinary actresses, available figures reveal an even more extraordinary situation in light of women's wages throughout the century. In the 1798-99 season, William Dunlap paid his various actresses weekly wages of $25, $37, $20, $14, $13, $12, and $16. In the next season, furthermore, the salaries of continuing actresses were raised.[69] Such popular stars as Mrs. Merry could even then, at the turn of the century, command from $50 to $100 a week.[70] And in addition to their regular salaries, most actors and actresses were allowed to hold about two benefit performances annually. The actress who held a benefit reaped most of its profits; she might net $500 to $1,000 annually from benefits alone.[71] As the century wore on, moreover, the salary of the actress improved, despite fluctuations in the national economy. Olive Logan reported that an ordinary actress in 1850 could expect from $40 to $60 a week, and a popular actress in good demand could command from $5,000 to $20,000 a year.[72] At mid-century, Lester Wallack's Theater in New York City was paying its male and female employees from $6.00 to $55.00 weekly, with guarantees of benefits written into the contracts.[73] Nor did this situation prevail only in the East. According to George MacMinn, a theater historian of the Far West, women took home immense salaries in the inflation-ridden frontier: the lead actress in a California mining theater could earn $200 a week in 1849, and amateur secondary actresses could earn $60 a week.[74] There is even an account of a Swiss organ girl who accumulated $4,000 in the course of five or six months on the California stage.[75]

In fact, the salaries of actresses in any part of the country were so good that the women were often preyed upon by unscrupulous men looking for small fortunes or steady incomes. Both actors and actresses repeatedly warned the young girls in the profession to be wary of prospective suitors:

> It is astonishing with what blindness and reckless disregard of results young ladies on the stage, after having by their industry acquired handsome sums of money that with their talents would make them independent, pecuniarily, for life, will throw away these blessings and destroy their comfort, perhaps their happiness, by bestowing their hands and fortunes on heartless adventurers who have nothing to recommend them, but, perhaps, goodly persons, and subtle tongues to plead their suits.[76]

The high-salaried Lucille Western, much in demand on both coasts, is a good example. Her husband certainly knew that he had a good enterprise in having married an actress, and he knew her income from night to night. It was his custom to gauge the house before one of his wife's performances, estimate the receipts within $5.00, and gamble it all away before her performance was over. During one session he managed to gamble away three nights of his wife's work.[77]

Even the lowly ballet girl often earned a sufficiently large wage to make her game for unscrupulous men. One actor, William Davidge, observed that "she at times unites herself to one whose means are not of that positive and satisfactory nature represented [in domestic dramas] and awakes to the fact when too late, to know that the evening of her life will be consumed in laboring for the support of him and his offspring."[78]

It is hard to refute the fact about theater economics that these figures unfold: this often disparaged profession offered women better wages than did other more "respectable" occupations. Even more unusual was the theater's custom of paying women salaries equal to those of men, for this policy of equality of payment in the theater prevailed at a time when gross inequality was rampant in other professions. In the 1840s, for instance, male teachers had average salaries almost three times those of female teachers.[79] In the 1860s female teachers were still paid only half of men's salaries.[80] In 1860 saleswomen in department stores were paid less than half the wages paid to men for the same work.[81] In the 1870s and '80s, women doing mill work were paid only half the wages paid to men, and in heavier, outdoor work the disparity was even greater.[82] In the 1880s and '90s, a male factory worker received $14 a week for performing the same work for which women were paid $4.[83] In any place, at any time in the century, one finds, as Matilda Joslyn Gage wrote in 1893, woman was "receiving less pay than man for the same kind and quality of work."[84]

By contrast, actresses and actors were paid on the same scale according to their talent in the company. Woman came closest to economic equality in the arts and especially in the theater, according to historians Vera Brittain and Elizabeth Dexter.[85] "Actress and actor," wrote Dexter, "advanced side by side."[86] Olive Logan, writing in the nineteenth century, was firmly convinced of this from firsthand experience: "An actress is a woman who, from the moment she steps her foot on the stage to the moment she leaves it, is in receipt of a salary as good as that of an actor of the same degree." In the theater, she noted, men and women "stand on an absolutely equal plane in the matter of cash reward."[87] When differences in salary did occur, they appeared to be based on differences in talent and public demand, not sex. If one performer were more valuable than another, he or she received more money, regardless of sex. Thus a successful actress very often took home much more salary than her male counterpart. Going to the records of William Dunlap's 1801 season in New York, one finds that Mrs. Merry, Dunlap's female lead, drew $100 a week, while the company's male lead, Thomas Cooper, drew $38.[88] Many times the wife of an acting team received more money than her husband, if she were more talented and popular. Two actresses, identified as Mrs. Seymore and Mrs. Johnson, for example, were paid more by the Park in 1800 than were their actor-husbands, also employed by the Park.[89] George C. D. Odell recorded a number of similar cases in New York throughout the century.

This unusual economic position of women in the nineteenth-century theater resulted in an extraordinary domestic situation for a number of them: they were the principal or only breadwinners in their families. Since the taboo against women working outside their homes limited most middle-class married women to domesticity, a large share of them lived in total ignorance of even the most elementary financial matters and were cared for by their husbands. If a woman did work, the inadequate salary paid her was scarcely enough for self-support. This situation and, of course, the power of traditional role assignment meant that one rarely found a female who was financial head of a household that included a male adult. Nevertheless, here, as in many other matters, the theater was the reverse of ordinary society, for in the theater many women were the principal or sole support of themselves and their families. Although the salaries of ballet girls were low compared to those of other women in the company, even many of these young people supported mothers, brothers, and sisters.[90]

Actresses, of course, could and did provide for themselves and their families much more easily than could ballet girls. Sometimes an actress supported herself and her husband after he had suffered financial reverses, as in the cases of Anna Cora Mowatt, Emma Wheatley, Mrs. Hackett, and Mary Ann McClure. It was the financial collapse of Mowatt's husband that drove her to the stage in the first place. Similar reverses necessitated the return to the stage of Emma Wheatley, an actress who had retired the year after she married the son of a bank president. In the eighth year of their marriage, his business failed, and she once again turned to the theater.[91] An actress identified as Mrs. McClure retired twice and returned twice in order to see her husband through financial crises.[92] Clara Morris tells a similar story of an actress named Sallie St. Clair, who supported her husband and two female invalids. St. Clair, in a moment of poignant confession, revealed both her success and his despair: "I always see my wife, Sallie, with a helpless woman over each shoulder, and myself on her back like the 'old man of the sea,' a pretty burden that for a sick woman to carry."[93] In some cases, when husband and wife were both performers, the actress-wife, seeing her husband's fortune fail as he lost favor with the public for some reason, emerged bearing the entire financial burden of the family. Such was the case of Mary Ann Duff. She and her husband, John Duff, had come to the American stage together from Ireland—he as a leading actor, she as a novice; but as his health and popularity waned, her career began to blossom, until ultimately they changed places. She became the sole support of herself, her husband, and their ten children.

It was not in matters of income alone, however, that women enjoyed equality of opportunity. The accounts of managers reveal that actresses as well as actors, if they were solidly entrenched as even modest stars, wielded significant influence in such matters as the selection of plays and the assignment of roles. And if one were a star of any magnitude, he or she enjoyed immense artistic and financial power. Charlotte Cushman reigned supreme over the companies in which she played, choosing her supporting players and the dramas to be offered. Less powerful women, like Adah Menken and Clara Morris, also had the influence to direct the ways in which scenes would be played, the persons to whom parts would be assigned.

These opportunities for economic and artistic equality and power on the part of the actress helped pave the way for another unusual custom of the time: the assignment of male roles, or breeches parts, to females. This practice, while dating back to the introduction of actresses to the stage during the English Restoration, was nevertheless so widespread and so endemically a part of theater at this time and place that Bernard Hewitt calls it a particular phenomenon of the nineteenth-century American stage.[94] If one dips into any part of the century, one commonly finds a woman playing Hamlet or Romeo or Puck or any number of other male roles from Oliver Twist to Cardinal Wolsey. The practice enabled a good actress, who could ordinarily only look forward to the parts of vaporous heroines who fainted and shrieked with regularity, to attempt the great tragic heroes of world drama, thereby partially compensating for the universal scarcity of truly good female roles. It also allowed her to expand her own artistic perceptions. Breeches parts, furthermore, were found in all parts of the country and in all kinds of theaters. It was, as a matter of fact, fairly rare to find an actress who did not at some time take a male role. The frequency of the practice did not quiet a few still, small storms of controversy which emerged from theater people as well as traditional moralists on the grounds that breeches parts were unnatural, immodest, and unwomanly. The charge of immodesty stemmed somewhat predictably from the often requisite display of legs: all Elizabethan and certain other historical roles called for the use of tights—at a time when the very word *leg* was avoided in many "moral" circles and even piano legs were sometimes skirted. Among the more vehement critics was the manager Noah Ludlow, who denounced breeches parts as "a series of Monstrocities" and "objects of disgust."[95] An actor, George Vandenhoff, deplored the very idea: "A woman in attempting it, 'unsexes' herself to no purpose. . . . She denaturalizes the situations, and sets up a monstrous anomaly. . . . There should be a law against such perversions."[96]

There can be little doubt, however, that any such law would have failed, for the public seemed to enjoy the spectacle. In fact, one of the odd hypocrisies of the day, as related by William Wood, was that, while the general public violently objected with some frequency to the costumes of female dancers, no matter how thoroughly and absurdly they bundled themselves up, audiences continued to support actresses in tights who assumed male roles.[97]

How breeches parts grew to have such importance at this particular time and place can be a matter of speculation only. Obviously one pertinent factor was the century's insatiable demand for novelty on stage. The same impulse that caused the public to flock to see five-year-old Kate Bateman play Richard the Third, or to see a stage full of trained horses and dogs, or *Julius Caesar* in blackface, most certainly drew it to continual appearances of women in men's clothing. Bernard Hewitt attributes the trend to the discovery of the female form and the desire to view shapes that in conventional settings were entirely hidden by petticoats and blouses. Hewitt also associates what he calls this "transvesticism" with a move toward equal rights and an emerging belief in equality of the sexes.[98]

Actually, explanations of why the century encouraged the trend are no more than educated guesses, but some of the reasons why actresses and theatrical companies promulgated it are fairly clear. The policy operated to the advantage of both player and company. The company benefited especially from the assignment of juvenile male roles to actresses. The maturity and skill required to play a young boy like Oliver Twist, for example, were beyond the scope of most young juveniles. The mature actress with a slight build would be more likely to make a success of such a part: she could easily be made to look like a boy, and her years of experience would enable her to bring needed skill and insight to the part. Thus, the roles of Albert in *William Tell*, the Dauphin in *Louis XI*, Patrick in *The Poor Soldier* and Puck in *A Midsummer Night's Dream* were frequently filled by actresses.[99]

The actress in turn, benefited from the greater number of parts available to her when women were cast as males, but especially from the opportunity to play the great male leads in dramatic literature. Classic plays in which a woman had the central role could almost be counted on the fingers, but the enviable male roles were inexhaustible. Most of the assignments of male *leads* to women, as opposed to male secondary roles, occurred in particular circumstances. One was an actress's benefit performance, when she could choose her own play and her own part. For a time at mid-century it appeared as though every actress in New York had chosen to play a male role for her benefit performance. Annie Hathaway played Richard III, Fanny Herring portrayed Richmond, Mrs. Battersby acted both Hamlet and Macbeth, and Mrs. Baldwin was cast as Marc Antony. Between 1821 and 1858 in New York City alone, at least twenty-six women played some thirty to forty male roles, including Cardinal Wolsey, Richard III, Romeo, Richmond, Macbeth, Marc Antony, and Shylock. [100]

Rose Bell. (George C.D. Odell, *Annals of the New York Stage*. Columbia University Press. Reprinted with permission.)

Alice Harrison.
(George C.D. Odell,
*Annals of the New York
Stage.* Columbia
University Press.
Reprinted with
permission.)

Another circumstance, besides the occasion of her benefit, gave an actress an extraordinary opportunity to play male leads: that was her undisputed position of power and influence in a company. When her talent and drawing power made her indispensable, she could play the coveted roles whenever she wanted, without benefit of benefit. In her long career, for example, Mrs. John Drew played the Duke of York, Dr. Pangloss, Richard III and many other male roles.[101] Adah Menken played the male leads in *Mazeppa* and *Black-Eyed Susan*.[102] Helen Weston, who was the star of her company, played almost as many male as female roles.[103] The same was true of Clara Fisher, who even cast herself as Shylock, and in boys' parts was said to be "unsurpassed."[104] Charlotte Cushman, the queen of breeches parts, took on every male lead imaginable, from Romeo to Cardinal Wolsey.[105] Laura Keene played Oliver Twist, David Copperfield, Romeo, Faustus, and the double male lead in *The Corsican Brothers,* as well as many others.[106] Always with one eye on the success of the entire production, Keene would take whatever role needed filling, whether it was male or female, major or minor. When Joseph Jefferson, a member of her company, refused to play Puck, Laura, with her usual adaptability, took the role herself.[107]

Thus, by virtue of the breeches part, the nineteenth-century actress regularly had artistic opportunities that have not been available to actresses in all ages. Curiously enough, the role reversal offstage for the actress who supported a family continued onstage when she played male as well as female parts.

The most dramatic evidence of the opportunities offered women in the theater—the power to create policy and to enter business—lies in the impressive numbers of women who actually managed theaters. This was at a time when the average wife remained fairly ignorant, not only of her husband's business, but of the simplest financial arrangements

Fanny Herring. (George C.D. Odell, *Annals of the New York Stage.* Columbia University Press. Reprinted with permission.)

of her own household, and when virtually none of the women in the work force assumed positions of authority. Yet in the nineteenth century a number of women in the theater were in full charge of whole companies of employees, responsible for all personnel decisions regarding both men and women. They were also responsible for other financial as well as artistic arrangements which made or broke their businesses. They determined salaries, saw that salaries were paid, arranged loans, bargained with landlords, paid for the physical necessities required to stage a production, and in some cases initiated and planned the construction of theater buildings. At the same time that other businesses and professions were closing their doors to women, the theater was slowly opening up these managerial positions to women as never before. Indeed, the nineteenth century was undoubtedly the age of the female theatrical manager. As early as 1844 the trend was sufficiently widespread to impel Joe Cowell, a comedian of the day, to label it disparagingly "petticoat government."[108] The initial impetus seems to have come from the career of the English actress Madame

Mrs. John Wood. (George C.D. Odell, *Annals of the New York Stage.* Columbia University Press. Reprinted with permission.)

Kitty Blanchard. (George C.D. Odell, *Annals of the New York Stage.* Columbia University Press. Reprinted with permission.)

Vestris, in whose London-based company Laura Keene had appeared. Many American actresses followed Vestris's example, notably Charlotte Cushman, Sarah Kirby-Stark, Catherine Sinclair, Laura Keene, and Mrs. Drew.

The earliest successful managerial careers enjoyed by women in America began, appropriately enough, in the less structured, less crystalized society of the Far West. Three women in particular emerged in this background as theatrical pioneers: Sarah Kirby-Stark, Catherine Sinclair and Laura Keene. Keene, it is true, achieved her lasting fame at a later time in the East, but all three women initially made their marks in the turmoil of the early gold-rush days. Kirby-Stark and Sinclair went on to make theatrical history in the West, permanently establishing their own fame while at the same time shaping the theater of the region.

The first of these, Sarah Kirby-Stark, arrived from the East in 1850. A consistent champion of melodrama, she had already become known, because of her success, as "Wake-me-up-when-Kirby-dies."[109] In March of that year, six months before California became the thirty-first state, she established one of the first theaters in the territory—the Tehama in Sacramento. In August, she abandoned it to open a theater in

Stockton, on San Francisco Bay, and in September returned to reopen the Sacramento Theater. In October, she became comanager of San Francisco's new Jenny Lind Theater, operating in competition with the American, the Adelphi, and a circus.

By 1850 more than forty thousand people had come to the gold fields, and San Francisco, the port for adventurers, was a swarming city of tents, shacks, and opportunists. During the following summer, 1851, Sarah Stark toured California, opening theaters in mining towns and returning periodically to appear in San Francisco. With her determination to give that city the kind of drama it craved, and her own background in melodrama, tempered by a devotion to quality production, she promptly won the wholehearted support of San Francisco. What the public wanted more than anything else was spectacle, and

Mrs. John Drew
reigned the longest.
(Harvard Theatre
Collection)

Felicita Vestali. (George C.D. Odell, *Annals of the New York Stage.* Columbia University Press. Reprinted with permission.)

Kirby-Stark was a master at staging it. One of her extravaganzas in the spring of 1852 was graced by a group of naiads who frolicked in several fountains before donning armor to march around the stage. In addition to such spectacles, the public wanted variety. She responded with high tragedy, low comedy, musicals, melodrama, and farce. She ran the gamut, often presenting a different play every night. Her willingness to satisfy the tastes of the audience was matched by her inexhaustible energy, for she also appeared in most of the plays that she produced. G. R. MacMinn, in his history of the California stage, paid high tribute to Mrs. Kirby-Stark and her actor-husband, James Stark, in his evaluation of their place in California theatrical history:

Always these two pioneers of the theater in the Golden State were welcome, always they were full of enterprise, eager to try new things. It was they who ventured the California premiere of *Coriolanus,* early in 1855. It was they who received in that same year this unexaggerated praise: "Certainly no professional artists have stronger claims upon this community. They were the first to render the theater in California an institution worthy of the support of an intellectual and refined public."[110]

In 1853, while the Starks were still flourishing in San Francisco, a new personality arrived on the scene, first as an actress at Maguire's Theater and then, only two months after her San Francisco debut, as manageress of the Metropolitan.[111] This exceptional woman was Catherine Sinclair, an individual who might never have made a contribution to theatrical history had she not met with one of those misfortunes

Annie Kemp Bowler. (George C.D. Odell, *Annals of the New York Stage.* Columbia University Press. Reprinted with permission.)

Miss Marriott as
Hamlet. (George C.D.
Odell, *Annals of the
New York Stage.*
Columbia University
Press. Reprinted with
permission.)

that so often drove nineteenth-century women to the stage. She had
been the wife of Edwin Forrest, one of the foremost American actors
of the day, and their divorce after a decade of marriage, each accusing
the other of adultery, created sensational headlines throughout the
country. Although her marriage had brought her into contact with the
American theater, she had had no career of her own in her ten years
of marriage. She was, after the completion of the trial in 1852, unable
to support herself, and for years after the divorce, Forrest managed to
maneuver out of paying the court-decreed alimony. Attempting to
make the best of a bad situation, in 1852 she borrowed the funds to
hire George Vandenhoff to train her and get her a few engagements
in the East—banking not only on her own ability, but on the notoriety
of the very public, very nasty divorce trial. She debuted in New York
as Lady Teazle in *School for Scandal,* and her gamble paid off almost
immediately. After her first few performances, the audiences, who had
come from curiosity, praised her abilities as an actress.

Shortly after her initial success in New York, she decided to go to
the Far West, hoping that that area's well-known disdain for convention
might ease her progress in the theater. She appeared first in San Francisco's Maguire's Theater in 1853 and began working for maximum

Catherine Sinclair, ex-wife of Edwin Forrest. (Harvard Theatre Collection)

exposure. She turned down no offer, made the rounds of every theater in the city, volunteered for every benefit, and, lest she leave some stone unturned, arranged to give public readings. MacMinn traced her activities in the late summer of 1853:

> Late in August she was giving Shakespeare readings at Musical Hall for the benefit of the Mercantile Library. Three nights later she appeared at the same place in support of the instrumentalists, Herr Hauser and Monsieur Pique. On two successive evenings in the next week she supported first Edwin Booth in his benefit at San Francisco Hall, then Murdock in his benefit at the American.[112]

Then, still planning carefully, in September, 1853, after only two months in the city, she leased the San Francisco Theater (eventually to be known as the Metropolitan), took the lead in her own first production, and hired a talented young man named Edwin Booth.

It was immediately apparent that Catharine Sinclair knew how to succeed as a theatrical manager, at least for a while. Once she had leased the theater, she became its supreme ruler. Her strengths at the outset, like those of Mrs. Kirby-Stark, were the ability to please her audiences and the imagination to produce a balanced and various program. She produced operas and presented ballets as well as plays of all kinds. No star who came to California in the lifetime of her theater failed to play at the Metropolitan. The careers of Matilda Heron, Laura Keene, Edwin Booth, and the Batemans were all enhanced by appearances there.

Her successes were financially solid at first. The receipts for the first year totaled $400,000. Unfortunately, what was a tremendous cultural success eventually turned to financial failure as superstars whom she had brought to the theater bled the company of its profits, and the operas that pleased her more than they did her public began to cost more than they brought in. Nevertheless, her brief reign was epoch-making for theater in the United States: she had not only introduced new stars, she had enlivened the frontier theater with quality productions, and she had proved that a woman could initiate and run a complex organization. In 1855 she left the California frontier, which she had conquered, for another frontier in Australia.

In the wake of Kirby-Stark and Sinclair came Laura Keene, the manager supreme in an age of female managers.[113] Those who have studied her contributions to the American stage seem to agree with DeWitt Bodeen that she "probably did more for the growth of American drama than any other single person in the nineteenth century."[114] Her brief two months as manager of San Francisco's Union Theater in 1854 and four months' management of the American in the spring and summer of 1855 were only apprenticeships for a big gamble in New York City that she began later that same year.

Her first bit of luck after returning from the West was finding the Metropolitan Theater up for lease. Once she had secured it, she redecorated and named it for herself. A running battle with other managers followed. They were unused to having a female competitor, particularly a newcomer who refused to defer to the theatrical establishment and who waged public wars against them in the newspaper columns. In light of her later skills at innovative advertising, one suspects that her continual acrimonious letters to the editor, attacking other managers, were a part of her promotional campaign. However, her theater was then plagued by vandalism that was difficult to pin on her adversaries, and this unpleasantness forced her to postpone the theater's opening. After it finally opened, her productions throughout the season met with great success. However, she had still not seen the last of obstruction from other managers, for at the end of the season she lost the building. Her lease had not been legally secure, and another manager was able to pull the building out from under her. George C. D. Odell attributes her difficulties in this first year to an eastern bias against women in managerial positions: "The brave lady fought an uphill fight, and won her public. The managers were against her, perhaps on the principle that so long kept votes from women. And when victory seemed assured, Miss Keene lost the theater on a technical quibble. . . . Those opposed to Laura Keene found her indomitable."[115]

Undaunted by this setback, she went right ahead with plans to have her own theater built. Laura Keene's Theater was a grand, comfortable structure, decorated in fine style with white and gold damask and satin. The newspapers called it the best in the city. As her theater went up, however, the Civil War was threatening. Businesses were failing right and left, and theaters all over the country were closing. Nevertheless, the originality and energy of Keene kept the theater lively even in these bad times. Part of her success is attributable to aggressive promotional tactics, often designed to anger other managers. She was shameless in her advertising. Often she would spread her publicity over half a news page and place numerous quips throughout the paper to draw attention to an upcoming production. She even staged elaborate fireworks displays in front of the theater.

Her contributions to all areas of stage management are important. She extravagantly and elaborately staged every production, making every effort to produce the grand effect with as little money as possible. She valiantly fought against the star system that was forcing the closing of many companies, but she paid her regular actors well, often wooing the finest performers away from their companies by offering them better parts and more pay than they were receiving from other managers. Edward H. Sothern and Joseph Jefferson were among those who graced her company.

Her greatest strengths were her tenacity and adaptability. When someone was needed to sew costumes, she became a seamstress. If a hand was needed to paint sets, she painted sets. She assumed whatever part was necessary to put on the show, often taking leftover male or female roles. She was successful in finding new plays and new types of entertainment when the old ones began to fail. In a particularly bad time, her adaptation of a new afterpiece called *The Elves* carried the company through its difficulties. At another time, a new play called

*The Love of a Prince* saved the season. When she, along with the rest of the country, faced sure financial ruin in the 1858-59 season following the great panic of 1857, she slashed prices and hunted madly for a play that would keep the company going. What she found was a melodrama called *The Sea of Ice,* which played for weeks. She refurbished another unlikely play called *The Seven Sisters* and was able to see it through 203 consecutive performances, the longest unbroken run in New York at the time. Her discovery of *Our American Cousin* was a major event in theatrical history. Only two plays in the century, *Uncle Tom's Cabin* and Barnum's *The Drunkard,* were more successful. Managers who had once done everything in their power to stand in her way were now borrowing her plays. "Barnum's," wrote Odell, "like many theaters, was reaping a second crop from the Winter Garden and Laura Keene's."[116]

Although she was British born and reared, Laura Keene made a concerted effort to encourage the development of American plays. Her policy was to introduce as much new material on stage as possible, as many new American playwrights as she could support—in short, to use the Laura Keene Theater for the establishment of a true American drama. The success of a number of playwrights, American and British, is attributed to the $1,000 prizes she offered for original plays. The most important playwright she sponsored was probably the Irish writer Dion Boucicault. It is clear that she did not operate in any kind of nationalistic vacuum, however. She was interested in contemporary European theater as well and became the first manager to hire scouts to apprise her of new plays and talent on the Continent and in England.

That Laura Keene's Theater stayed open in the most difficult of national times—it was the only legitimate theater open in New York during the summer of 1861—is a testament to her extraordinary managerial skill. Odell gives her a special place of importance in his history of the American theater. Her years as a manager, he says, form "one of the bright chapters in the best of our drama."[117] The demise of her theater came during the Civil War. Odell, always dependable as a candid and discriminating reviewer, wrote, "A poem of epic proportions should have marked the exit."[118] For the remainder of the war and for four years thereafter she toured the country with her company, for a time directing the Chestnut Street Theater in Philadelphia and finally ending her career as a manager in a last abortive comeback in New York two years before her death in 1873. Her career, like those of many other theatrical women, stands as a brilliant example of high accomplishment and achieved potential in a man's world—a world of which the large majority of women in her age had no knowledge whatsoever.

The theater establishment in cities other than New York seems to have been consistently more hospitable to female managers. In 1860 the stockholders of Philadelphia's Arch Street Theater asked, not Mr. Drew, but Mrs. Drew to assume the management of their theater,[119] and that was the beginning of a career of great success and longevity. In her autobiography, Mrs. Drew made a special point of mentioning that her husband was out of the country, in Australia, at the time she received the stockholders' business proposition. When Mr. Drew returned from touring, he became a member of his wife's company. She retained control of the Arch Street from 1860 to 1892, retiring finally at the age of seventy-two. When she first assumed control of the theater, she was prepared to borrow funds to attract the most talented actors available, and borrow she did—for every week of her first season. As a result, business improved; she began to pay back the company debts; and the stockholders, in the second season, agreed to build a new theater for her. By the fourth season, she was able to employ figures of the magnitude of Lester Wallack and Edwin Booth.

After eight years of operating a highly successful repertory system, she gave in to the pressures of the star system that had engulfed Philadelphia. The Arch Street eventually suffered, as did all theaters, from this continual drain on finances. She also struggled consistently to compete with larger theaters in the city. Nevertheless, with Joseph Jefferson, her sole attraction toward the end, she, as manager, held the Arch Street together through the years. In 1880, at the age of sixty, she took a company on a nineteen thousand-mile tour. Amazingly enough, she managed the Arch Street even while she was on the road and kept it going until 1892 when she retired from management.

These women and others like them did meet with vocational successes in the nineteenth-century American theater—success they could find in few other places. But it is important to remember that for most of the great actresses and manageresses, the theater was not a romantic lark or even an artistic mission: it was an economic necessity. The motivations of actresses in particular, as they are revealed in memoirs and biographies, were accurately reflected in 1857 by Moncure Conway: "A few persons go on the stage from genius and strong inclinations; many more because they can get employment there; by far the majority are there simply to get a living, and if they should have fortunes left them, would not remain."[120] This is certainly illustrated in the lives

and writings of many actresses, at least up to the Civil War. Anna
Cora Mowatt began reading, then acting, in public only after her
husband's financial ruin. After a long career, she left the stage when
it appeared that she would no longer need to support herself, feeling
"some decided attachment for the profession," but certainly no "passion" for it.[121] Olive Logan, born of a theatrical family, was much more
outspoken in her assertion that economic necessity alone kept her on
the stage:

> For myself, I am free to confess that I never liked the life of an actress.
> My mature judgment rebels against it, *for me*, as much now as it did when
> I was led on, against my infantile wishes, to personate Cora's child in the
> play of *Pizarro*.
>
> I know that this is equal to an acknowledgment to actors that I had not
> the sacred fire for dramatic art; and I candidly believe I never had.
>
> It was necessity which drove me to it in the first place, necessity which
> at different intervals in my life sent me back to it; and I trust such necessity
> will never come upon me again.[122]

Fanny Kemble, too, actually hated acting from the first—hated it
while she was a star and hated it when she had to return to it. Her
letters and journals suggest that one of her chief reasons for marrying
was to be able to leave the stage behind.

Despite the actress's frequent failure in artistic fervor, she found in
her profession artistic and financial status available directly to women,
but less tangible benefits were also hers—independence, freedom, and
a profound dignity that could only come from self-esteem and self-
accomplishment. Wives at home and women in other jobs were largely
the servants of other people. From this servitude the actress was spared.
As Clara Morris maintained, the actress might even say that she, of
all other women, worked for herself:

> The actress's independence is comparative; but measured by the bondage
> of other working women, it is great. We both have duties to perform for
> which we receive a given wage, yet there is a difference. The working girl
> is expected to be subservient, she is too often regarded as a menial, she is
> ordered. An actress, even of small characters, is considered a necessary part
> of the whole. She assists, she attends, she obliges. Truly a difference.[123]

In spite of Olive Logan's distaste for acting, she also felt and cherished
that independence and dignity that Morris saw in the profession. The
idea of being able to depend on herself was to Logan as important as

having a salary. The actress, she wrote, did not have to marry merely to have her "board and lodging paid"; she could support herself, "feel when she lies down at night that she is really thanking her Maker and not her husband, for having given her this day her daily bread."[124]

Several generalizations can be made about those actresses who found a place in the profession. First, they assumed the economic responsibility, usually accorded to males only, of supporting themselves and their families. Second, they assumed this burden more often from necessity than from choice. Finally, many actresses, especially the most successful, had unusual or very unhappy marriages or engaged in no courtship or marriage at all. A glance at the lives of some of these women, so different from each other in many respects, illustrates how their common vocation made them citizens of this extraordinary subculture in their century—one that expected of women the independence so untenable in society at large.

To select, from a field of many women, only seven actresses as illustrations of the high achievements possible in the profession is to invite controversy. William Winter, outspoken historian of the nineteenth century, would certainly have disagreed with my omission of Ada Rehan. Furthermore, those interested in what was called the emotional school of acting of the 1880s and 1890s would certainly have included Clara Morris and Matilda Heron, as this study does not. There are others whose contributions and popularity give one pause: Helena Modjeska, a Polish actress who introduced Ibsen to the United States; the highly popular Clara Fisher, Mary Anderson, Adelaide Neilsen, Julia Marlowe, and Maude Addams, most of whom appeared on the stage in the last two decades of the century; and the notorious Lola Montez, known to have caused a civil war in Europe and to have horsewhipped an editor.

There is, however, a clear line that separates these figures from the seven women selected for inclusion in this study. One can present strong arguments that most of the seven were far better actresses than their contemporaries. However, the important difference is not entirely one of quality. It might be explained better in this way: History signals us that, unlike those of their sister actresses, both the individual appearances and the entire careers of these seven were unmistakable *events* in theatrical history. Their lives and their careers made headlines in their own time and have subsequently found places in history. All had extraordinary public appeal and talents that gave them a star quality far brighter than that projected by other women of their day. Each is spoken of in superlatives, as an innovator of considerable importance.

Mary Ann Duff is included because she is the first superior trage-dienne of the American stage. Her biographer, Joseph N. Ireland, is convinced that no other actress in the century approached her quality. Although there is debate over the claim that Charlotte Cushman was the finest actress of the nineteenth century, no one would deny that she dominated the American stage for years. Her power was indis-putable. Fanny Kemble's career was brief but brilliant. Her arrival in the United States was one of the most heralded events in theatrical history in that she was believed by many to be the first real challenger for the title so long held by Mary Ann Duff. Her illustrious family, her own star quality, her highly publicized failure to reconcile her career with her marriage, and her articulation of that problem kept her in the public eye for most of her life. Anna Cora Mowatt's career was the most meteoric and rigorous of any in the century. She also distinguished herself in theatrical annals as the creator of *Fashion*. Laura Keene's supremacy is also self-evident. She could at least *lay claim* to the title of the greatest theatrical manager of the century. George C. D. Odell said that no one made a greater contribution to the American stage than did Laura Keene. No claim at all can be made for Adah Isaacs Menken's greatness as an actress; on the other hand, no more brilliant personality ever graced the American stage. She also found the acclaim in Europe that was so rarely forthcoming for Americans, and her association with the grand literary figures of England and Europe contributed to her legendary flamboyance. Adah was one of those stars who became known by one name only, "The Menken." Another such star was Charlotte Crabtree, known from coast to coast simply as "Lotta." From her emergence as a child star in California until her retirement, she was the preeminent star of American broad comedy.

These seven women are not, then, presented as average individuals, nor even as average actresses. Instead, one sees, often magnified in their lives, the character of the profession: the changes it required in the typical domestic life of the time, the problems it created, and most important, the achievement it made possible for women. In sum, one sees vividly set forth in the lives of these actresses the heights to which woman could climb in an outcast profession.

# CHAPTER 3

# MARY ANN DUFF

Mary Ann Duff (1794-1857) was the first great tragic actress in nineteenth-century America. Although she was British by birth and rearing, she arrived in the United States as a sixteen-year-old bride. It was here that her career really began, and here that she remained for the rest of her life. Here she was buried.

A strong argument can be made for her supremacy as a tragedienne of the nineteenth-century American stage. The great actors of her day, including Edwin Booth and Edmund Kean, praised her in superlative terms. Booth called her the greatest tragic actress in the world, and Kean, who also acknowledged her superiority, paid her the high compliment of asking her to modify the force of her characterization when playing opposite him so that she would not detract from his performance. Even after the advent of Charlotte Cushman and Fanny Kemble, John Gilbert proclaimed that she had no superior. Joseph N. Ireland, her biographer and a stage historian with considerable knowledge of actors, seems never to have doubted for a minute that Mary Ann Duff was the best tragedienne in nineteenth-century America. In his eyes, Kemble and Cushman would challenge her position, but no one would equal her.

The life of this woman of such unquestionably great achievement lies in relative obscurity. Even in her own day she was regarded as a person of mystery. Except for a few scattered comments by

In old age Mrs. Duff embraced the church and buried her old identity as an actress. (Joseph Ireland, *Mrs. Duff*)

stage professionals who crossed her path, most of what we know of Mary Ann Duff comes from one biography by Ireland. Even his materials are few: records of performances, a few letters and poems, passing comments by other actors, theatrical reviews in newspapers. There are great gaps in the record of her professional life and few hints about her private life. What is known of her, however, forms a fascinating picture of paradoxes, and supports the generalization that most nineteenth-century actresses viewed their work as an economic necessity rather than as a means to artistic fulfillment or personal glory.

Mary Ann Dyke was born in 1794 and moved to Dublin from England with her family in 1809. Fame was seemingly a negligible consideration from Mary Ann's youth onward. Legend has it that the poet Tom Moore, who eventually married her sister, first paid court to Mary Ann without success. Instead, she became Mrs. John Duff at the age of fifteen, choosing, rather than the illustrious poet, a poor Irish actor. Soon afterward, in 1810, the two of them went to America, where he sought a livelihood.

Before she met John Duff, Mary Ann had already made a humble beginning onstage in the Dublin theater as a dancer. For many years after the Duffs' move to America, her career remained quite unremarkable. She began her career in America playing secondary roles in Boston's Federal Street Theater, which was obliged to hire her in order to have her husband. After two years in Boston, the Duffs joined the company of Warren and Wood in Philadelphia. They were one of numerous acting couples who lent respectability to theatrical companies. To this end their names appeared on the program as "Mr. Duff" and "Mrs. Duff." Most of the roles that came her way were not ones for which she was well suited. Despite her weakness as a comedienne, she was assigned light parts, since Mr. Wood gave all the serious roles to his wife. Because of her slim, youthful figure, Mary Ann also played the parts of young boys, appearing in *The Blind Boy* as Edmund and in *Deaf and Dumb* as Julio. In 1817 the Duffs moved back to Boston to join the Boston Company, where John became comanager.

In these early years neither Mary Ann nor the companies in which she worked regarded her efforts very seriously. Her husband was the professional; she seemed to tag along reluctantly for the additional income needed by their rapidly growing family. This attitude is shown in W. B. Wood's recollections of the year 1811. The old manager praised John Duff for his ability to increase the company's profits, but his estimate of Mary Duff was not high: "Mrs. Duff at this time was very pretty, but so tame and indolent as to give no hope of the improvement we afterwards witnessed."[1]

The most remarkable thing about Mary Ann Duff during the years of her marriage to John is not so much her lack of enthusiasm for her profession as the fact that she continued on the stage at all, for in those twenty years she bore ten children. How the many pregnancies and problems of attending to infants affected her vocation is a mystery. Ireland, writing at a time when such matters were considered too delicate for discussion, could make only veiled references to stretches of time when she was unaccountably absent from the boards. He drew attention, for example, to five years from age nineteen to age twenty-three when she apparently did no acting. Then she appeared for a year, only to absent herself again. "The Boston season commenced October 11, but Mrs. Duff's appearance was delayed until the 31st of December. . . . After two or three representations of the drama Mrs. Duff was again absent from the stage until the eighth of May, 1820."[2] In January 1822, a long illness of some kind again kept her from any stage appearances, and from August 18, 1822, to April of 1823, there is no record of any performance by Mary Ann Duff.

Except for these absences, when she was undoubtedly confined by various of her ten pregnancies and bouts of ill health, Mary was a sporadically active performer in theater companies, a fact recorded in playbills and newspaper advertisements of the day. William Winter indicated that an incomplete list of the characters played by Mary equals 220. So, while records suggest an early failure to take her profession very seriously, they also show that she persisted, despite the domestic demands of a large family.

As she approached her middle twenties, however, during the five-year absence of 1812-17, her attitude toward acting apparently changed. This hiatus represented a turning point; afterwards she began to merit the attention of reviewers by bringing greater energy and precision to her work. She started for the first time to master the mechanics of her trade, and her voice had become powerful and well disciplined. By the middle of the 1817-18 theater season, when she was twenty-four, she was getting considerable attention in the press and being praised highly for her performances in Shakespearean tragedy as Juliet, Romeo, Desdemona, and Ophelia. From 1817 on, her rise in the profession was swift and sure, attributable to a growth in insight as well as discipline and skill. As she toured the Northeast, reviewers noticed a depth in her representations that they had never before expected of her. In 1823 a reviewer for the *Boston Gazette* observed this growth: "Hitherto she has lacked animation; but this season, especially during the engagement of Mr. Kean, she has burst from our dramatic constellation like a celestial stranger. She has evinced new powers and has proved that she is possessed of talents which must raise her to the foremost rank of her profession."[3] Her career blazed like a meteor that year. No longer was she restricted to unsuitable comedy roles or boys' parts. No longer was she an afterthought in her husband's company. By as early as 1821, she had played opposite the most renowned actors of her day. She had also gained sufficient pride in her work to refuse Kean's request that she play with less force during their appearances together. Her only professional failures during the 1820s were with the New York theatrical establishment, which scorned her as it did other "stock" actors from "out of town," and a disappointing engagement at London's Drury Lane in 1828. C. D. Odell called the former failure "the disgrace of New York and the unsolved problem of the antiquary."[4] New York's attitude toward Mary was typical of its chauvinism in dealing with any actor from the provinces who had not risen through the ranks of New York theaters.

The account of her career from her arrival in America to the 1830s raises more questions than it answers, in particular the matter of what caused the change in her attitude toward her work after the long absence. One possibility, not suggested by Ireland, is plausible in the light of what we know of other actresses and of Mary Ann's early disinterest: that is, that Mary Ann's five-year absence was not an "interruption" in her career; rather it may have been intended as a longed-for retirement from the stage—a retirement so frequently begun with hope and so often ended when she was driven back onstage by the family's need for money. Mary Ann Duff's return to the stage and the new energy she brought to her work might conceivably have been motivated by an awakened professional ambition; nevertheless, records like this account from the *Boston Gazette* indicate that her heart never fully belonged to her work:

> We trust her benefit may be fully attended, for, added to her professional merit, she has a charm which never fails to please with our fair country-women—the charm of a virtuous life. She is known to be the kind, careful, and pious mother of a numerous family, and it is said by those who are best acquainted with her, that if the public awaken her professional ambition, the endearments of her family have all her heart.[5]

The likelihood is that she returned to the stage from necessity. Her husband had embarked on a risky venture as manager of the Boston Theater and desperately needed her help as an actress. Her determination and discipline in her craft was very likely the result of her having seen the handwriting on the wall. Ireland wrote that she already sensed in 1818 what began to be apparent to theater and press alike by 1824—that her husband, John, was failing as an actor and suffering reverses of all kinds from which he would never recover:

> It has been surmised that anxiety for her family was the chief cause of Mrs. Duff's awakened energy and desire to excel in her profession, which in earlier life she had felt unnecessary and had been indifferent to. In the beginning of their career in America, Mr. and Mrs. Duff were both very attractive, she from personal loveliness, and her husband from his excellent acting. Their salaries were fair and their benefits most liberal, but Mr. Duff's management at Boston had been profitless. Kean, the Wallacks, Booth, Maywood, and other lights had dimmed the brilliancy of his achievements as an actor. He did not advance in excellence, and from repeated attacks of gout he was frequently on the sick list for weeks in succession. Mrs. Duff felt that on her alone would soon depend the entire support of her family, a fear that in after years was unfortunately realized.[6]

By 1824, then, there had been a complete reversal of their former roles, a reversal of the traditional roles of nineteenth-century husband and wife. Ireland, without any comment on the obvious import of his simple observation, said merely that, although Mrs. Duff played at times with Kean, Booth and other stars, it was her husband who played the supporting male roles for most of her appearances. Only a few years before, he had been the star, and she had been the reluctant tagalong. From what we know of her early lack of enthusiasm for the stage and her subsequent eagerness to leave it, it is highly unlikely that Mary Ann Duff took any joy in the reversal of the family's vocational situation.

By 1825 the public and press had become aware of symptoms in her husband's career that she had probably sensed approaching for some time. Reviewers were merciless in scorning what they interpreted, not so much as failing powers, but as carelessness and sloppiness—their comments sounded ironically like manager Wood's estimate of Mrs. Duff's early "indolence." The reviews, damning him while praising her in superlatives, must have made painful reading for them both. As

Mrs. Duff as Mary in *Superstition*. (Library of Congress)

early as 1825 John was publicly scolded for his lack of effort. Nevertheless, he continued acting and continued being compared with Mary until bad health forced his retirement from the stage. An *Albion* barb of 1827 illustrates the harsh reviews that the couple continually endured: "It would be judicious in Mrs. Duff to persuade her husband to make himself master of his author. His forgetfulness and inaccuracy on Tuesday were shameful."[7]

MR. DUFF.

*AS MARMION*

Engraved by A.B.Durand from a painting by J.Neagle.

Lopez & Wemyss' Edition.

Published by C.R.Peale Philad.

1826

The failure of John Duff's health forced a reluctant Mary Ann to continue on the stage.
(Library of Congress)

By the end of 1827, his stage appearances began to be extremely rare. Her activity, on the other hand, had to increase as his waned, and she took on more frequent touring engagements. A review in the *New York Mirror* for May 5, 1827, after Mrs. Duff's season at the Park Theater, sums up the public view of the actress:

> This lady is decidedly the best actress in our country. We have for a long time intended to speak of her in a separate article, and more at length than the limits of a notice of the performances through the week would permit. The subject, however, is one of difficulty. There are few who are not able to appreciate good playing; but there are fewer who are capable of conveying to the mere reader anything like a distinct idea of an actor's merits. To Mrs. Duff, in particular, this observation applies. In her style of acting there are none of those prominent points—none of those strongly marked characteristics, which are of such service to the dramatic critic, in his observations on the stage. Mrs. Duff has one great characteristic; one peculiarity that strikes all who see her, and that is, UNIFORMITY OF EX-CELLENCE. She makes no points, We cannot say of her as we used to say of Kean, "that is a beautiful touch." Her merits and defects (though the latter are few in number and trivial in amount) pervade the whole of whatever character she undertakes. There is no singling them out. . . . From beginning to end, from her first entrance to her final exit, you see before you only the characters she is personating. The unity of her con-ception—THE ONENESS is remarkable. No temptation can induce her to break it. If a scene offer ever so much opportunity for display, and it be a display not authorized by the whole design, end, and tenor of the part, she suffers it to pass by unembraced. This is the perfection of her art. . . . She seems to have a separate existence, during the continuance of the play. . . . Kean used to startle us by electric flashes—Mrs. Barnes occasionally shines out with great brilliancy—but Mrs. Duff pours out one unceasing blaze during the whole time she occupies the stage. We do not mean to say that there is uniformity of interest in all she says and does, but a uniformity of excellence. [8]

Soon after John Duff's forced retirement, the public became aware of the couple's situation: John's illness and the impossible economic burden which rested on Mary Ann's shoulders as the sole breadwinner of their large family. Ireland's quotations from newspapers show that the press had unusual fondness for Mary Ann, encouraging the much-needed support of her benefits, taking pains to draw attention to "the cares and anxieties of her home life added to the tasks of her stage avocation" which "would seem sufficient to depress the most active spirit."[9] In early April of 1831, when the necessity of working was most acute, she quit performing to nurse John. On April 28 he died. Within a month she began acting again to support her children and herself. The apex of her career, one of the most illustrious of the nineteenth-century, was the lowest point in her private life. She was in abject poverty and mental despair, unable to depend on her children, who were more of a hindrance than a help. She fast accumulated huge debts and bad credit. Her miserable economic situation and the opium to which she had long been addicted, taken as a remedy for her delicate health, seemed always ready to plunge her into nervous collapse. Certain actors, including James E. Murdock, knew of her addiction and de-scribed her personality at this time as always amiable, but nervous.[10]

Two years after John's death, she involved herself in a bizarre incident to escape the stage and free herself from impossible financial burdens. This singular incident is one of the few things remembered and recorded about her by theater historians. In 1833, a Mr. Young appeared at her house to claim her as his wife and to announce their previous marriage. Mrs. Duff refused to acknowledge him as her husband. Soon records were produced by Young to prove that he and Mrs. Duff had indeed been married shortly before his announcement—not in just one, but in two different ceremonies: both Catholic and Protestant. He had, he reported, initially agreed to a three-year period of separation before the marriage would be consummated, but he had changed his mind and called to claim Mrs. Duff as his wife only a few days after the cere-monies. Mary Ann finally admitted to the public that what Young had announced was true, that she was, in fact, married to him. Ac-cording to Young, the idea for the marriage had come about when he had walked her home one evening—the full extent of their courtship. He had proposed marriage to her upon reaching her door, and she had accepted. After the incident was made public, Mary Ann had the marriage annulled on the grounds that opium had temporarily caused her to lose her senses. She announced that she was "persuaded to take this step while in a temporary alienation of mind produced by opium taken during a season of illness and severe domestic sorrow."[11] A friend of Mrs. Duff's, Mrs. Charles Durang, explained the situation to Ireland:

> Mrs. Duff was overwhelmed with debts accumulated by the extravagance of her family. In an unfortunate moment Charles Young beheld her dis-traction and offered his hand to her to aid her, representing that he had just fallen heir to a large property in England, which he would settle on her children if she would accept him. Maternal affection prevailed, con-

ditions were agreed to, and the ceremony was twice performed. Scarce were the ceremonies over when he confessed the imposition he had practiced, that he was not worth a cent, and that the provision she had made—not to live with him for three years—was a simple nullity. Her brain could bear no more; reason gave way—when Mrs. Ewing went on to New York and brought her to Frankford, Pennsylvania, where she continued to reside till her mind was sufficiently restored for her to resume her profession.[12]

It was typical of the nineteenth-century actress, even the most successful star, to look for a way out of her profession through marriage to a man of wealth. This was the unfortunate road taken by Fanny Kemble and Anna Cora Mowatt, both of whose marriages ended in disaster. For years, even before John's death, Mary Ann had been in deep financial trouble. With widowhood these problems doubled. Some of her children were old enough to be helpful, and had she been able to depend on them for whom she had sacrificed so much, her anguish would certainly have been less. But such was not the case, as Ireland wrote:

Disappointed and disheartened with the result of her year's labors, embarrassed in her pecuniary affairs, involved in debt by the extravagance of her family, and painfully affected by the recklessness of some of its members, Mrs. Duff had now fallen into a state of despondency verging on insanity.[13]

The failure of her children to support her in her desperate need of a home is reflected in the following letter, which she wrote to Mrs. Durang in March of 1834. She describes her situation and wishes that Mrs. Durang's children will be kinder than her own. The Matilda mentioned in the letter is Mrs. Duff's daughter:

Dear Madam—I trust you will pardon me again for troubling you, but Matilda in her last letter again forgot to mention her place of abode. I addressed a letter to her last week which is not answered; I suppose it yet lies in the office. Mr. Isherwood run off this morning in everyone's debt. I wish to return home when it may please my children to let me know where that home is.

Give my love to your mother. I hope you and the children are all well. That they may bring you comfort is the fervent wish of

Your friend, Mary Ann Duff[14]

Mary Ann Duff's financial and domestic worries did not lessen until she met a Mr. Seaver, sometimes called Sevier, of New Orleans, to whom she became engaged. He began covering her debts many months before they were married in 1836. Finally she was able to leave behind both her financial worries and a career for which she had never betrayed any fondness. For a few years thereafter she was able to "know where home is."

For two years she made occasional appearances on the New Orleans stage in support of charities. A performance in 1838 to raise money for orphans was probably her final one. After three decades of an intense and successful theatrical life, she joined forces with the enemy of the theater, the church, displaying the unwavering devotion of a convert. Her life was thereafter devoted to her home and her church: Sunday school, prayer meetings, missionary societies, and temperance organizations. She did whatever she could to put her life as an actress behind her. She not only refused to make any further appearances herself but discontinued playgoing. "She avoided players and playhouses and seemingly strove to forget that she had ever been among them."[15]

In 1854 she and her husband disappeared from New Orleans. Ireland reported that, as long as the couple lived in that city, they seemed to have been compatible. But William Winter wrote in *Wallet of Time* that she "ultimately became unhappy in marriage."[16] In any case, they both disappeared for about twenty years. Eventually those interested in her history found that she was living in New York City with her daughter. What had happened to her husband was and still is a mystery. In these last years of her life she remained a shadowy recluse. Winter described her as "a sad, subdued, broken-spirited old lady." Even those who visited in her daughter's house were ignorant of her past identity as America's leading tragic actress.

In an inexplicable and curious way, the anonymity of her final days was continued after she died of cancer in 1857. Her death and her daughter's came within a few days of each other. Their bodies were laid in the receiving tomb of Greenwood Cemetery on September 6, 1857, and on April 15, 1858, they were buried in the same grave. The burial certificate bore the words, "Mrs. Matilda I. Reillieux and Co." The "and Co." was Mary Ann Duff. The grave marker bore an equally anonymous "My Mother and Grandmother." The reason for this curiosity is never given by her biographer, but William Winter offered this explanation: "There seems to have been a purpose to conceal the identity of Mrs. Sevier with Mrs. Duff, and to hide the fact that the mother of Mrs. Reillieux had ever been on the stage."[17] Another stage professional, Noah Ludlow, attributed the peculiarity to "sectarian prejudice." "It seems that both mother and daughter had used their best endeavors to conceal the fact that Mrs. Sevier had ever been an actress."[18]

The pathetic irony of Mary Ann Duff's existence was that she had the exceptional boon of fame, even adoration, but all she ever seemed to have wanted, she could not have—a home for herself and her family. Her poems, copied by Ireland, indicate that her idea of heaven on earth was simply a home. One of the poems is entitled "On the Prospect of Being Homeless":

> Grant me a hut near pastures green,
> and near a small, clear-flowing stream
> That every morning when I wake
> I there my mortal thirst may slake
> But let thy house, O God, be near
> That I the word of truth may hear
> And free from care and worldly strife
> Drink of the waters of eternal life.

She wanted only the tranquility of anonymity—to be the hidden flower in the poem "Impromptu to a Wild Violet":

> Pretty violet, child of the shade,
> O that like thee I had been made
> To dwell in some secluded glade.
> And there unknown to bloom and fade.
> Oh! how I love the forest wild,
> Where the woodland-dove cooing mild
> Mourns no lost nor absent child.
> She with her brood and loving mate
> Is more blessed than queenly state
> Ever made woman whose fond heart
> Is doomed from all she loves to part.
> I know one who from youth was bound
> From year to year to bear such wound,
> She lives—if breath gives lie, seems cold, is proud,
> Nor speaks her many griefs and wrongs aloud.[19]

What she wanted was a home. What she got was theatrical fame. The stage, publicly understood to be the enemy of the family, was the only thing that stood between her own family and starvation for most of her life. It saved her, but just barely. It was a shelter she did not want. It rewarded her existence when nothing else would, and she took the meager reward from need, not love. It heaped fame on her that she did not particularly want. The paradox throws an interesting light on the end of her life, making more of a puzzle than ever of her conversion and of the firm, deliberate wiping out of her past. It is as if for the first time in her life she had a choice, and that choice was a denial of all that she had ever been.

# CHAPTER 4

Pub.ᵈ Feb.ᵈ 1830 by T Gillard, 48 Strand London

MISS FANNY KEMBLE.

Drawn by E. F. Lambert

# FANNY KEMBLE

By all rights Frances Ann Kemble (1809-1893), the darling of audiences in England and America, should have felt completely at home on the stage. Her father's family was a six-generation, English theatrical dynasty. Her father's sister was the glorious Sarah Siddons, believed by many people to be the greatest actress produced by England. Fanny's Uncle John and her father, Charles, were two of the most famous Shakespearean actors of the day. Her mother had gone onstage at the age of twelve in order to support her widowed mother, brothers, and sisters. Such was the theatrical tradition into which Fanny, a special star in the Kemble galaxy, was born in 1809. It was reported that she inherited her father's dignity, her mother's courage, and the family talent; but she neither inherited nor developed any love for the stage.

Several things very likely contributed to Fanny's distaste for the profession of her ancestors. The exclusive Parisian school to which her parents sent her until she was nineteen taught her a love of music and art but surrounded her with a class of people who believed that actors were unsavory characters, coarse harlequins at best. Her religious education undoubtedly did little to contradict that view of the profession. She would always remind herself that an actor's life was a shameful pretense. The bad luck that plagued her father as manager of London's Covent Garden Theater also made her associate shame and

This painting of Fanny Kemble suggests her independence and spirit. (Library of Congress)

93

unhappiness with the theater. Throughout her childhood the household buzzed with Covent Garden's troubles—threats of bankruptcy and closings kept the family in turmoil. The threatening din from rioting patrons who objected to price increases may have reached her ears as a child. It requires no psychiatrist to see that these continual conflicts caused the young Fanny to associate the theater with unhappiness and instability. The theater also interfered with the young woman's desire for domestic happiness—a husband, children, and cultivated friends.

How, then, did she end up as an actress of such prominence? This outcome was certainly not of her own choosing. It took a combination of events to place her on the stage—a trick of fate, a crisis, coming at a particular moment in her youth when she was still passive, an object, an instrument to be used. The crisis occurred when she was twenty years old, the year after she had returned home from boarding school. Covent Garden, which had been in the family ever since Fanny had, was cursed from the beginning with debts and depressions. One day in 1829, while her father, Charles, was on tour in Ireland, Fanny's mother rushed into the house in hysterics. On her walk home, she had passed by Covent Garden and seen "for sale" bills posted on the outside of the theater building. The revelation caused Fanny to feel "seized with a terror like the Lady of Shalott, that 'The curse is come upon me.'"[1] She knew that she would now have to go to work. Even in what was a desperate situation, however, she seems never to have thought of the stage as a vocational possibility. Instead, she determined to look for a position as a governess—about the only work available for the "respectable" educated woman.

Her family had a different plan for her life. Her mother was the first to see that a new Kemble onstage was the remedy for the economic ills of the family. By the time Charles returned to do battle for Covent Garden, his wife had listened to Fanny read and was ready to approach him with a plan: Fanny would be groomed for a stage debut. She would be the means by which the Kembles and Covent Garden Theater would be saved.

Almost immediately upon Charles's arrival the entire family began preparing Fanny as the instrument with which disaster would be averted. In three weeks her mother trained her for the part of Juliet. At the same time, her father prepared to play opposite her in the role of Romeo, and her Aunt Dall became her personal guide in the theater, preparing her dress and makeup, calming her down when she began weeping before her first appearance and, finally, with the rest of the family, literally pushing Fanny onstage only three weeks after rehearsals began.

Her debut did save the theater temporarily. She was a heroine. Even Sir Walter Scott paid tribute to her "active support" of her father.[2] Her biographers regarded the rescue of the family theater as much more of an unhappy sacrifice on her part. Fanny Wister wrote that "her family accepted as a matter of course that she should become the galley slave of Covent Garden in their last attempt to save themselves from ruin."[3] Margaret Armstrong, another biographer, also regarded Fanny's debut as tragic: "There is no doubt that Covent Garden Theater, in failure and in triumph, was the pivot around which the family fortunes turned all through Fanny's babyhood and childhood and, when the final crisis came, her girlhood was sacrificed to Covent Garden in much the same matter-of-course fashion that St. George's princess was thrown to the dragon."[4]

Even at the time, no one saw her as a determined Joan of Arc. Any picture of a strong-willed girl, taking the fate of the family firmly in her hands and making a selfless decision to step into the breach, is an inaccurate one. She was less a heroine than a useful tool, a passive object being manipulated—benevolently perhaps, but still used. Passively, if fearfully, according to Armstrong, she did what she was told: "She spoke, curtsied, moved this way and that, smiled or wept, put on a frock or took it off, like a child anxious to please."[5] Beneath the surface, if we can judge from her journals, was neither a purposeful martyr nor a disinterested child, but an intelligent, quiet girl who felt a decided aversion to her work and her surroundings. She remembered later that as she was being prepared for her first stage appearance— coached, dressed, and observed—she felt as if she were being led to her execution:

And so my life was determined, and I devoted myself to an avocation which I never liked or honored, and about the very nature of which I have never been able to come to any decided opinion. . . . I never presented myself before an audience without a shrinking feeling of reluctance, or withdrew from their presence without thinking the excitement I had undergone unhealthy, and the personal exhibition odious.[6]

Other quotations throughout her journals show that despite the first night's financial success, the parental pride, the applause from the public, and her theatrical background, she felt morally tainted by the pretense of her profession:

My going on the stage was absolutely an act of duty and conformity to the will of my parents, strengthened by my own conviction that I was bound to help them by every means in my power. The theatrical profession was, however, utterly distasteful to me, though acting itself, that is to say, dramatic personification, was not; and every detail of my future vocation, from the preparation behind the scenes to the representations before the curtain was more or less repugnant to me. Nor did custom ever render this aversion less; and liking my work so little and being so devoid of enthusiasm, respect, or love for it, it is wonderful to me that I ever achieved any success in it at all.[7]

Nevertheless, a success she was and an instant one at that. She was lionized, immediately thrown into the lively social scene throughout England, and in 1832 her fame was sufficiently secure as to earn her the double honor of starring in a play, *Francis I,* that she had written at seventeen. Yet despite the social and artistic successes—both the result of her stardom—the good times for Covent Garden, hence for the family, were short-lived. Political unrest, an epidemic of cholera, and a depression again spelled the end of the family theater. All the thousands of pounds that Fanny had earned in her few seasons had been invested in the theater and lost. The salvation of Covent Garden had turned out to have been only a staying action, not a solution, and the family once more faced disaster. For a second time a plan was conceived to use Fanny to regain the family's fortunes: she, her father, and Aunt Dall would go to America. The plan jolted her because it would not only prolong her hated career upon the stage but also necessitate a family separation. Still, real fortunes were to be made in America, especially by English stars. A proven veteran like Charles Kemble and a new and attractive young Kemble, who had received rave notices in the English press, could reap all the rewards.

Her father's predictions were right. No other event on the American stage was so heralded as the arrival of Charles and Fanny Kemble. W. B. Wood, a famous actor and manager in the American theater, recalled their American engagement as a special event: "The arrival of this gentleman and his gifted daughter, recalled the enthusiasm which Cooke and Kean formerly excited, and their performances amply realized the high expectations of the audience."[8] Philip Hone's diary of his years as mayor of New York is the source for an account of the audience reaction to Fanny Kemble's appearance in his city:

I predicted before we went that it would be no half-way affair; she would make the most decided hit we have ever witnessed, or would fail entirely;

and so it proved. I have never witnessed an audience so moved, astonished, and delighted. Her display of the strong feelings which belong to the part was great beyond description, and the expression of her wonderful face would have been a rich treat if her tongue had uttered no sound. The fifth act was such an exhibition of female powers as we have never before witnessed, and the curtain fell amidst the deafening shouts and plaudits of an astonished audience. She has some faults: her low tones are sepulchral and indistinct—and yet her voice appears to me capable of anything which her judgment would lead her to execute—and she is at times somewhat monotonous, particularly in the unimpassioned passages; but this may be the defect of education. It was the fault of John Kemble and of Mrs. Siddons, and is that of her father. . . . But on the whole I am quite satisfied that we have never seen her equal on the American stage, and England has witnessed none since Miss O'Neil.[9]

One of the younger members of the audience who saw Fanny Kemble's first performances in New York would attribute the flowering of his own poetic genius at least in part to Fanny Kemble's power as an actress. Walt Whitman remembered his youthful impression of her performance as an important influence on *Leaves of Grass:*

Fanny Kemble! Name to conjure up great mimic scenes withal—perhaps the greatest! . . Nothing finer did ever stage exhibit—the veterans of all nations said so, and my young heart felt it in every night she played at the Old Park—certainly in all her principal characters. (Strange—but certainly true—that her playing, and the elder Booth's with Alboni's and Bettini's singing, gave the first part of the influences that afterward resulted in my *Leaves of Grass.*[10]

The great success in America and the financial windfall that came with it were still not enough to teach her to like her career. At a time on her American tour in Philadelphia when she was receiving high praise and the highest wages reaped by any actress on the American stage, she thought again of her hatred of a vocation that she had never chosen of her own free will. The letters she wrote from Philadelphia in 1833 leave no doubt about her lack of enthusiasm for what she was doing. Her disgust smacked of a puritanical distrust of the imagination. In fact, her youthful tirade could well be taken for a sermon attacking the stage:

How I do loathe the stage, these wretched, tawdry, glittering rags flung over the forms of ideal loveliness, pitiful substitutes for the glories of poetry. Pasteboard and paint for the thick breathing orange groves of the south; green silk and oiled parchment for the solemn splendor of the moon at night; an actress, a mimicker, a sham creature—*me,* in fact—for that most wonderful conception, in which all that is true in nature, and all that is exquisite in fancy, are moulded into a living form. To *act* this! to *act* "Romeo and Juliet." Horror, horror, how I do loathe my most impotent and unpoetical craft![11]

Everything made her regret this life devoted to the stage. When in 1834, Dall died as a result of a carriage accident, Fanny thought of how her vocation had robbed her of time she could have spent with family members. They had always been first in her thoughts, but, in fulfilling her duty to them, she was separated from them.

By the time of Dall's death, however, Fanny had matured from a passive child into a young woman who was beginning to make her own choices. She had been forced to take many matters into her own hands, to manage finances, engagements, and living arrangements. These duties had multiplied when Dall's accident occurred. Fanny then made all the plans to have her cared for and got the money together to meet her medical expenses. Charles sat helplessly by after Dall died, leaving to Fanny the burdens of making arrangements for the funeral and for their subsequent traveling. Fanny's independence of action was now matched by her independence of thought. She had no reluctance about expressing her opinions—particularly her opinions of America. She did not hesitate to disparage American culture and manners. She publicly scorned what she found to be a false sense of delicacy and hypocrisy. American women were neither complimented nor pitied when she called them drudges as housewives and nonentities as socialites.

In 1834, two months after Dall's death, she made one of the hardest decisions of her life: to leave a lucrative career over her father's violent protest, contrary to the best interests of her family in England and in violation of her dead aunt's wish that she choose a career instead of marriage. Marriage had been on her mind for some time, probably ever since she left school; nevertheless it had occurred to her during her four-year career that marriage might not be right for her. In addition, Aunt Dall, herself a spinster, had urged her to put aside marriage indefinitely in order to devote her life to a career. Fanny recorded on July 22, 1831, a conversation in which Dall told her that, as long as she remained single, she would have "an independent and ample" fortune. And Fanny herself was aware of certain distinct advantages "which I cease to own when I give myself away." Not only would she "lose everything," but marriage would be "incontrovertible and not so pleasant." Despite the doubts and the ambivalence, Fanny did marry and did leave the stage. The suddenness and the determination behind her action, in the face of so much pressure to the contrary, leave the unmistakable impression that her ultimate desire was to enjoy domestic bliss. Furthermore, her continual interest in children and her lifelong philosophy about the proper life of women as wives and mothers suggest that she always thought of a happy marriage as an aim of her life.

Fanny Kemble did not want a career. She did want a marriage, and she had fallen in love. For several months before her decision in 1834 she had been in love with Pierce Butler, a wealthy southern planter, who seemingly had all the social graces and also had been "paying court" to her for two years, ever since her arrival in America. He had actually volunteered to play the flute in her orchestra just to continue at her side wherever she went. He was charming, and he gave the impression of having a great deal of money—a house and land near Philadelphia and a southern plantation. Some observers believed that she had fallen in love conveniently, having for some time been negotiating for the richest husband. And Pierce was a Prince Charming in more ways than one; he would, she thought, give her the opportunity to have her own secure and graceful home, to have children, and to escape a life she disliked. In April of 1834, she wrote: "I did not expect to remain on the stage after the month of May, when my marriage was appointed, and I hoped to be free from a profession which has always been irksome to me."[12]

In light of her father's violent opposition to her decision to leave the stage and marry, the stand she now took was particularly traumatic because she adored her father and had always been completely subservient to him. She also knew for a certainty that her marriage would be the end of Charles Kemble's career, since his popularity and skill had been in decline for some time and he now needed a strong supporting actress. When they returned to New York from Boston in April of 1834, the conflict between the two became intense. It was at this time that she announced her decision; she intended to enter into an engagement with Pierce. The most that Charles could hope for was a postponement of the marriage. Finally, a compromise was reached: at her father's insistence, Fanny would delay the marriage for a year

Fanny Kemble as a reader. (George C.D. Odell, *Annals of the New York Stage*. Columbia University Press. Reprinted with permission.)

in order to continue acting. She would then turn over to him all her savings, the earnings accumulated in America. Had she not given the money to Charles Kemble, it would have reverted, of course, to Pierce upon their marriage. When Charles returned to England that spring, Fanny did not join him as they had planned, but his coffers were fat with the money she had drawn from numerous savings accounts. With her father so far away, she now gave in to her own wishes. Supported by Pierce, she broke her promise to her father, broke her contract with the Park Theater, and married in June of 1834. She, whose bank accounts had overflowed only months before, came to her marriage without a cent. Nor was she able to replenish her savings. Evidently

Pierce had assured her that she could finish out the year as an actress, but once they were husband and wife, he insisted that she leave the stage for good.

Fanny's longing to quit the theater in order to have a family led to a disastrous marriage. She had been warned in a general way about Pierce Butler when they were courting, but because she was in love and eager to change her life, she apparently failed to read his character accurately. She had never seen his way of life, his plantation, or much of his family. It took almost no time at all after she married him for her to discover him to be tyrannical, profligate, and indolent. Even his reputed wealth was not what she had been led to believe. Everything Pierce had called his own was actually a fortune he had not yet inherited and for which he had never done anything except change his name, a condition of his maternal grandmother's will. For all practical purposes, he was no wealthier than she. In addition, the fortune-to-be was almost totally in land and slaves. His slave holdings were in fact among the three largest in the United States, numbering in the hundreds. But all the land and all the slaves did not automatically produce a life of grace and comfort. If Fanny had envisioned an elegant, garden-surrounded estate in the English style, she was sorely disappointed. The residences actually were rundown and primitive.

Fanny's marriage spelled the end of her stage career for fifteen years, but the examination of these fifteen years of marriage is valuable as stark contrast to the life of the female theater professional. Fanny had eagerly moved from an institution in which she had exercised the rights accorded male professionals into an institution in which she had no rights at all. Another young girl, sheltered and inexperienced, might have found a marriage such as this neither surprising nor intolerable. But to one who had been a strong-willed, self-supporting professional, a marriage to Pierce Butler was one of constant affront and perpetual frustration. The stage had ill-prepared her to be a wife. She never recognized that the reasons for her success in one endeavor and her failure in the other may well have resided in the institutions themselves—one accorded her comparative equality and dignity as a human being, and the other did not. Paradoxically, she always despised the generous institution and applauded the restricting one.

Pierce's and Fanny's differences were many, immediately apparent, and all related to her refusal to become a passive, empty-headed, "ideal woman." The marriage was under a strain as soon as they came home from their honeymoon to share a house with Pierce's relatives in Philadelphia. These staid, narrow-minded people were dismayed at her high temper, her boredom within the house, her passionate singing, and her love of color, among other things. Furthermore, Pierce forbade her to entertain people of her choosing, like her old theater friends, Mr. and Mrs. Charles Matthews. From this first episode in the beginning of their marriage until the divorce, Fanny's friends were a bone of contention. He would not tolerate actors in their household and violently expressed his displeasure with Fanny's friends, such as Elizabeth Sedgwick whom he accused of being "free thinking."

Another crisis arose over her insistence upon publishing a journal of her impressions of America written during her first two years here. Although Fanny had when she was single sold the journal to Carey, Lee and Blanchard, Publishers, Pierce had been under the impression that she would withdraw it at his request after their marriage. After a battle, Fanny got the journal into print, but only with Pierce's heavy-handed editing of it. With its appearance in the United States, his predictions that it would harm her reputation came true; Americans generally classified her as another unladylike Englishwoman who had been an unfair judge of American manners. Fanny's criticisms of America were just as sharp and candid as Frances Trollope's. The general belief was that she had "unsexed" herself by exposing her opinions. Ladies, it was said, should be seen and not heard.

Her possible motives in making an issue over publication of the journal are interesting clues to her attitude toward the stage and her own independence. At the time of its conception, long before her marriage, the journal would have been an alternative income to the stage. After her marriage, she may have thought of it not only as a source of money but as a psychologically independent act.

She left Pierce for the first time after they had been married only a few months. It was one of several brief separations in a union that lasted for fifteen years. However, the worst conflict between the two did not begin until 1839 after the birth of a daughter, when she first saw her husband's Georgia plantation on a dark December day. The trip was depressing and uncomfortable; the landscape was ugly and bleak; and the house itself seemed to her scarcely habitable.

It had no plumbing and was provided only with pegs on which to hang clothing. The only furniture comprised rough-hewn pieces made by slaves. The land itself was unlandscaped and unimproved, desolate and malaria-ridden. Instead of flowers and trees, she found giant weeds. The single edible vegetable grown on the vast acreage was cabbage.

Plantation life brought about serious disagreements between the two, and inspired a journal for which Fanny would one day be as well known as for her stage career. Very likely there was more of Fanny's pride and love in this record of slavery, which grew out of her misery, than in all her stage performances.

She did not fill the traditional role of southern wife and mother while she was in Georgia. Julep-sipping on the veranda, afternoon siestas, visits and gossip with wives of other planters were hardly her métier. Instead she threw herself into activities on the plantation that were unthinkable for a white woman. She set up and worked in hospitals for blacks. She intervened on behalf of individual slaves who pled their cases before her. She defied the law by teaching slaves to read, and she published antislavery articles. Her leisure was as much a local scandal as her work, for she relaxed by galloping through the woods on horseback.

The gossip of whites who ostracized her and the excoriations of Pierce would have made life hard enough, but Pierce's other women made Fanny's life in Georgia a nightmare. Her life did not improve when he moved her abruptly to Philadelphia without forewarning, nor when he took her to England for a visit in 1840. They remained in England for three years, during which time Pierce lived like a lord and refused to pay his bills. Even the reports of economic disaster in the States failed to stop his extravagance. Fanny felt absolutely helpless. The least she could do was to try and pay their past-due bills by her writing, but Pierce threatened to use his legal prerogative as her husband to confiscate her earnings for his own use. Despite his threats, she was finally allowed to pay the bills with the publication of a ballet, *Pocahontas,* the translation of a Dumas Play for Covent Garden, an article on Victor Hugo, another on southern life, and a five-act play.

Fanny was aware that Pierce continued his infidelities during their stay in England. Perhaps this was one reason why in 1843 she begged to return to America where at least her marriage would not be under the scrutiny of her family and old friends. When Fanny and Pierce arrived home, they were forced to live in a boarding house in Philadelphia until the dilapidated country home in Pennsylvania could be made livable. Just after the move to the country, Pierce created a public scandal that was the beginning of the end of the marriage. To Fanny's horror, the husband of one of Pierce's mistresses published the details of his wife's affair with Pierce and challenged him to a duel, in which, incidentally, no one was wounded. Fanny had obviously thought of divorce long before this public humiliation, but she had hesitated each time relations between herself and Pierce worsened because, no matter what had been the extent of his adultery, the law as a matter of course would give him their two daughters. Even after this notoriety, she decided that remaining in an intolerable marriage was preferable to losing her children.

She soon discovered her helplessness; she had no choice in the matter, for Pierce concocted a plan that would force her to leave him. He decreed that she could remain in his house and see her children only if she signed a document agreeing to conditions that he set forth: she was no longer to communicate with anyone about matters within the household; she was never to refer to the past; she was to agree to turn over the training of her daughters to his mistress whom he had hired as a governess; she was to see her daughters for no more than two hours a day; she was not to communicate with Pierce except in writing; she was to remain restricted to her suite of rooms within the house; she was not to publish anything; and she was to receive no more than £800 a year.

After she had endured eighteen months of this life, Pierce entrapped her by sending her a letter from her friends, the Sedgwicks, with whom she had been forbidden to communicate. When Fanny opened the letter, she was considered to have broken the contract. In the fall of 1845, after a year and a half of living up to the terms of the intolerable agreement, she was forced against her will to leave her residence and live in a boarding house, comforted a little by the belief that Pierce would not be as harsh with the girls now that she was gone. She remained in the boarding house for only a few weeks before sailing to England, still legally married to Pierce but denied access to house and children, thrown out without an allowance sufficient to live on.

In England with her family in 1845 and on visits with friends in Italy, she pondered how she could support herself. She tried her hand as a writer, resisting even the idea of returning to her former profession. Her distaste for the stage was so persistent that she even went so far as to refuse a command performance in England. At about this time, William Macready surprised the theatrical world by announcing in his biography that he disliked actors and shielded his children from them. Fanny wrote to a friend that her own dislike for the stage was much more basic than Macready's: "How curious it seems to me that he could care, as he did, for his profession, having none of the feeling of dislike for it in itself that I had."[13]

The need for money, however, forced her to face reality: she could make a good living by going back on the stage. At her father's insistence, she began to act again, but she reserved small rebellions for herself. She refused to wear the new stage makeup or to appear for curtain calls, and continually announced to the world that her only wish in life was to make enough money to quit acting for good. Her attitude notwithstanding, the monetary return was good and her reviews were respectable. The high point of her reluctant return to acting was an invitation from Macready to play an engagement as his leading lady. Even though she was flattered by the honor, she had good reason to dread the actual ordeal, for Macready rarely failed to maim his leading ladies in the process of his violent performances. Their appearances together in *Othello* were highly successful, and Fanny counted herself fortunate in having paid only the price of a broken finger for this boost to her career.

In 1848, after only two years of stage appearances in England, she hit upon an idea that seemed much more suitable for one of her temperament. She would give up acting for good and attempt to support herself by giving readings of Shakespeare. The new venture was much more to her liking and, incidentally, much more profitable. Her preparation for the readings was minimal because she simply took over from her father, who had been doing the same thing. She even used his cuttings and arrangements.

In the summer of 1849, just as she became eager to return home to work out something with Pierce in order to be with her children, she received word from America that her husband was suing her for divorce on grounds of desertion. Immediately she canceled her engagements and went home to face a highly publicized divorce trial. Pierce's arguments were based on insubordination—in the matters of her journals, her conduct on the Georgia plantation, her defiance of his social conventions, her finding fault with his "governess," and her spying on him. She withdrew any defense of herself in exchange for some protection of her children's patrimony. The conditions of the divorce ensured that some property would be saved for the children, that Fanny would be given a small allowance, and that she would be allowed one month's visit with her children—not one month annually, but one month total, until they were free to leave Pierce's household. In September of 1849 the divorce was final.

Except for the loss of her children, whom she would not have with her for seven years, Fanny's life was full and pleasant. Her career as a reader had been a great artistic and financial success in America. On occasion, for example, she grossed $8,000 a month. At the same time, she enjoyed what she was doing, since she did not attach the moral stigma to readings that she did to other stage performances. For the first time, from her new home in Lenox, Massachusetts, she could relish the stimulating intellectual and social life of New England that, even as a girl reading William Ellery Channing, she had longed for. The Longfellows, the Lowells, Emerson, and Oliver Wendell Holmes were among her friends. Fanny became an accepted member of New England society without ridding herself of the unfeminine independence and eccentricities that had shocked Pierce and his friends.

Here in New England, she was tolerated, but it cannot be said that she was universally admired. A letter written by Herman Melville, her neighbor, and an excerpt from a work by Joseph Adams Smith show that Fanny's defiance of the feminine stereotype offended even these men of the world. After attending one of Fanny's readings, Melville wrote the following appraisal:

> Mrs. Butler too I have heard at her Readings. She makes a glorious Lady Macbeth, but her Desdemona seems like a boarding school miss.—She's so unfemininely masculine that had she not, on unimpeccable authority, borne children, I should be curious to learn the result of a surgical examination of her person in private. The Lord help Butler. . . . I marvel not he seeks being amputated off from his matrimonial half. [14]

Joseph Adams Smith had a similar, unsympathetic impression:

> It was not to be supposed that many of the graver people would look with much complacency on the *port* and the demeaner of so singularly spirited a lady, much less on her man-like propensities to driving, hunting, and fishing, and less than all on her man-like attire, while engaged in them. [15]

One of the timely issues that held Fanny's attention during the New England years was "the woman question." Of course actresses were in the work force, and many of them had considerable influence and independence, but rarely did any of them openly support feminism. Fanny is one of the few who expressed an interest in the condition of women. As a girl she had noticed and deplored the life of women of her class in England, who referred to men as "our earthy disposers"; and one of her earliest observations on coming to America had been that "married women are either house-drudges or nursery maids, or if they appear in society, comparative cyphers." She did support women's suffrage, believed that any profession should be open to women, and wrote and spoke privately of the necessity for better education for women, particularly since they were, as she thought, at a physical disadvantage. But beyond this, she did not support the cause of women's rights. She had no sympathy for the feminists whom she knew or read about, partly because, she admitted, she lacked a full understanding of the issues. She realized the irony in her hostility and speculated about the reasons for it in a letter to her friend Harriet St. Leger: "I suppose my own individual superabundant sense of independence, and the unfortunate circumstances which have given full scope to its exercise, prevents me from sympathizing, as I ought, with the clamorous claims of the unfair sex in this particular."[16] Despite her own failure as a wife, she remained firmly convinced that woman's proper calling was to be wife and mother. According to Fanny, women were limited biologically; nature gave them the duty to bear and train children, and their physical inferiority to men meant that no civil law could possibly counteract the natural law that made them subservient.

By the time the children joined Fanny, her fortunes had reversed. She was wealthy from hard work, while Pierce had lost just about everything he had through mismanagement. It was she who was able to buy the mortgage on Butler Place in Georgia, all that was left to her daughters of the vast Butler estate. She lived to a comfortable·old age, supported by friends and on excellent terms with her children, who stayed with her until they married.

Her relationship to the stage was, like Mary Ann Duff's, a strange one. The American stage offered both of these English-born actresses a means of survival when nothing else did. Neither had ambition as actresses, yet almost in spite of themselves they rose to the top of their professions. Each yearned for the tranquil domesticity that the ordinary woman of the century enjoyed. Each was thrust unwillingly out of simple family life into extraordinary fame. Ironically, of all the things that Fanny attempted in her life, including acting, writing, and public reading, she failed at the only one her heart desired—marriage. As Fanny Wister wrote: "Fanny Kemble can be seen as a complex woman whose varied gifts and moral fiber made it mandatory that she magnificently fulfill several roles in life. Marriage was not one of them."[17] Although she died a quiet death after a tranquil old age, the vigor of her life is illustrated in a letter she wrote earlier, describing how she wanted to die: "The death I should prefer would be to break my neck off the back of my horse at a full gallop on a fine day."[18]

# _CHAPTER 5_

# CHARLOTTE CUSHMAN

Charlotte Cushman (1816-1876) is a study in contrasts. She, more than any other actress of the day, arrogantly defied the basic idea of what a nineteenth-century woman was expected to be; yet she seemed obsessed with social proprieties and hungry for social acceptance. Hers is one of the more interesting stories of what it was like in the nineteenth-century to be both a woman and a professional.

Unlike most other actresses of the time, Charlotte Cushman was born into an upper-class family. It was well known that her ancestors, old New England stock, claimed to have come to America on the *Mayflower*. The family into which she was born was affluent as well as aristocratic. Unhappy circumstances, however, placed the high-born young girl in the same position of most other women who went on the stage; like them, she entered theatrical life from necessity, because she found herself shouldering a large burden which, as a woman, she was unprepared to bear. When she was thirteen her father's business failed, and she was compelled to leave school. Shortly afterward, he died, leaving his family in poverty. The unexpected hardships of her girlhood, particularly heavy for one who had known nothing but comfort and security, was an experience that left lifelong scars. In later years she wrote that the poverty had robbed her of her girlhood. Another effect was certainly her concern with the

Cushman in her later years. (George C.D. Odell, *Annals of the New York Stage.* Columbia University Press. Reprinted with permission.)

accumulation of money. She never seemed to have enough to dispel the specter of that sudden poverty of her youth. She could not get out of her head the early fear that her mother, whom she supported all her life, would kill herself from despair over their poverty. Probably as a result, she later became an especially shrewd businesswoman who made all her own financial arrangements, trusting no one but herself. Like Laura Keene, she drove a hard bargain and advised other actresses to do the same. She had the reputation for being tightfisted, even to the extent of refusing to give friends passes to her performances. The shrewdness and parsimony cultivated as a result of her poverty led to the accumulation of an estate worth half a million dollars at her death.

However, when she was thirteen, there seemed to be no way out for either Charlotte or her family. After her father's death, the rest of the family turned to her to support them because she was strong and responsible. Two conditions dictated the decision to solve her problem by taking music lessons: her extraordinarily good voice and the belief that the stage was one of the few places where an untrained woman could find work. Her initial plan was to work in stage musicals, not straight drama, and while in her early teens she got a position in a musical company run by James G. Maeder in her native Boston, eventually leaving with the company on a tour to New Orleans. Here she faced a turning point in her career: her singing voice failed her, and she left her musical role with the Maeders for an acting one—the part of Lady Macbeth, which had become available at a New Orleans theater. Speculations vary about just what happened to her voice. Unsympathetic historians believe that Charlotte planned the failure to take advantage of what she saw as an opportunity for a starring role. She herself reported that Maeder was responsible for the loss of her voice: in order that his wife could have all the contralto parts, he had forced Charlotte to sing in a high register, unsuited for her. Whatever the cause, she was an actress and not a singer from that time on.

Records of these early years reveal that Charlotte had little hesitation in going onstage—no moral scruples, no trace of the fear of social ostracism that almost paralyzed Kemble and Mowatt and that was certainly to be expected in the case of a Boston Brahmin like Cushman. When the opportunity to take an acting job presented itself in New Orleans, she jumped at it. If her uneasiness with her profession is betrayed in any way, it is in her clamoring to rise out of the social class in which actors found themselves.

As early as her girlhood years in Albany, she was hungry for the life of a socialite among the most prestigious members of any community—a position unheard of for an actress. Before she had any reputation as an artist, she managed to maintain a lively social life by playing hostess to state politicians. She jokingly said that more legislators went to her benefits than to the capitol in Albany. For all the rest of her life she would prefer the very wealthy pillars of society to the company of stage people. Every minute not demanded by the stage for rehearsal and performance was spent in paying calls, receiving callers, and giving and going to dinners, parties, and teas. She took great pride in displaying large numbers of calling cards, which were showered on her wherever she went. James Murdock, a fellow actor, classified her as a social snob. "Miss Cushman," he wrote, "was by nature and education a lover of place and position, of 'the ribbon and the star.' . . . Her fondness for society was insatiable, and wealth had no more devoted worshipper."[1] Her preference for high society was also evident in her professional life. She was not interested in seeking the approval of middle-class Americans; she preferred the British and upper-class American Anglophiles like herself. So she never encouraged American playwrights as did the British-born Laura Keene, and she rarely ever performed in American plays. Her uncommon success as a socialite, of course, may be partially attributable to her family background. In any case, some historians write of Cushman bringing respectability to the profession—surely a narrow definition of the word.

She received her first long-term engagement as an actress at the age of nineteen at the Bowery Theater in New York City. The experience began and ended in disaster when the theater caught fire, burning up everything including an expensive wardrobe that she had borrowed money to buy. Her career suffered a setback, but she immediately got another position in Albany, New York. Charlotte lived in Albany for only five months, but she claimed that two traumatic experiences occurred here that changed the course of her life, closing to her the usual avenues taken by nineteenth-century women and causing her to be totally devoted to her craft. The first was bitter disappointment in a suitor with whom she had fallen in love. When she discovered that his intentions were "not honorable," she stopped seeing him. She never fell in love again, never felt that she could again extend herself emotionally as wife or lover, as she explained in a reflective account written much later in life:

> There was a time in my life of girlhood when I thought I had been called upon to bear the very hardest thing that can come to a woman. A very short time served to show me, in the hard battle of life which was before

me, that this had been but a spring storm, which was simply to help me to a clearer, better, richer, and more productive summer. If I had been spared this early trial, I should never have been so earnest and faithful in my art; I should have still been casting about for the "counterpart," and not given my entire *self* to my work, wherein and alone I have reached any excellence I have ever attained, and through which alone I have received my reward. God helped me in my art-isolation, and rewarded me for recognizing *him* and helping myself. This passed on; and this happened at a period in my life when most women (or children, rather) are looking to but one end in life—an end, no doubt, wisest and best for the largest number, but which would not have been wisest and best for *my* work, and so far for God's work; for I know he does not fail to set me his work to do, and helps me to do it, and helps others to help *me*.[2]

Her second trial in Albany came after the death of her young brother, a surrogate son, in a horseback-riding accident. This incident also caused her, she wrote, to focus her energies more sharply on her craft:

Then after this first spring storm and hurricane of young disappointment came a lull, during which I actively pursued a passion—my art. Then I lost my younger brother, upon whom I had begun to build most hopefully, as I had reason. He was by far the cleverest of my mother's children. He had been born into greater poverty than the others; he received his young impressions through a different atmosphere; he was keener, more artistic, more impulsive, more generous, more full of genius. I lost him by a cruel accident, and again the world seemed to *liquefy* beneath my feet, and the waters went over my soul. It became necessary that I should suffer *bodily* to cure my heart-bleed. I placed myself professionally where I found and knew all the mortifications in my profession, which seemed for the time to strew ashes over the loss of my child-brother (for he was my child, and loved me best in all the world), thus conquered my grief and myself. *Labor* saved me then and always, and so I proved the eternal goodness of God.[3]

The "mortification" of her profession which she speaks of may refer to her dissatisfaction with the respectable, but not enthusiastic, reviews that she received in Albany and which prompted her to leave her starring roles in this provincial company for a theater where she would receive better training. She took a three-year position as a utility actress in Edmund Simpson's Park Theater in New York City. As an actress at the Park she played over one hundred twenty new parts in three years and lavished great care and industry on each small and insignificant role.

At twenty-three, after her three-year contract at the Park was up, she played at Burton's theaters in Pennsylvania and New York and returned for a starring engagement at the Park. Probably taking her cues from other successful women, she wanted to open her own theater. Ever since Albany, she had been supporting her mother and her brothers and sisters and very likely needed more money than an actress could make. She did manage the Walnut Street theater in Philadelphia for a while, but the plan to become a manageress was a failure. She had been able to keep working, but her career had come to a standstill. It is indicative of her good judgment and strength that she did not continue to drift along unproductively but took her life firmly in her hands.

At twenty-eight years old, in 1844, she decided to sail to England. There she sought out further training, taking William Macready as her model, and waited patiently and firmly for precisely the offer that would propel her career onward. Her decision was to hold out for star billing. It was an expensive journey and an expensive three-months' wait, but the plan worked. When she did appear, she was an immediate theatrical and social success. From this time until her death, she was at the top of her profession both in England, where she stayed until 1849, and in America. She had all the money, power, and attention that she craved. She played every part, male and female, that any actress could aspire to. Meg Merriles was probably her most famous role, but the list of characters in which she excelled, including all of Shakespeare's tragic heroines, is long.

Upon her return to America, she starred in every quality theater in New York: the old Broadway, Brougham's Lyceum, the Astor Place Opera House, Burton's Theater, and Niblo's Garden. A southern tour in 1850 was typical of the success she had wherever she went, reaping nightly profits that exceeded even those of the illustrious Macready. She was, on the basis of her fame and success in tragedy, comedy, and melodrama, the first person in the theater ever named to the Hall of Fame in the United States. She remained active until 1852 when, at the age of thirty-six, she gave the first of many farewell performances because of declining health. By 1869 she was in constant pain, sure now that her physical ailment was cancer. Indeed, part of the reason she continued to act long after her announced retirement was to keep her mind off the pain. She died of cancer in 1876.

By far the most unusual thing about Charlotte Cushman's personality and career was her lack of what were called feminine characteristics

Cushman as Meg Merrilies. (George C.D. Odell, *Annals of the New York Stage*. Columbia University Press. Reprinted with permission.)

and her preference for male roles. In the first place, Charlotte was not born with the delicate features that were then classified as feminine. She was considered by many to have harsh, large, therefore "masculine," features. Furthermore, her gestures and movements were rough and broad, inconsistent with the prevailing notions of femininity. Her voice was also decidedly gruff and deep. Many male actors were offended by what they considered to be her masculinity. Edwin Forrest, who was her costar for her first London appearance, said that she was not a woman, let alone womanly. And John Coleman, another actor, gave this description of a rehearsal for Romeo:

She had mounted a man's hat and coat, a man's collar and cravat, Wellington boots, which, so far from attempting to conceal, she displayed without reticence or restraint, as she strode about, or tucked up her petticoats, before she "polished off" Tybalt or gave the *coup de grace* to County Paris, or when she took "the measure of an unmade grave" at rehearsal. . . . These masculine proclivities shocked the spinsters in the company, and provoked satirical comment amongst masculine admirers or detractors, who incontinently dubbed the new Romeo "Charley de Boots." The desire evinced by la grande Charlotte to disport herself in masculine attire led to speculations which it would be indecorous to repeat here.[4]

She seemed to have accepted her masculinity easily and candidly. As a child she thought of herself as a tomboy; as an adult she wanted to be a man. Emma Stebbins, her biographer and close friend, commented extensively on what was interpreted as Charlotte's boy-like high spirits and love of mimicry, consistent with the account of a childhood friend who recalled a meeting in which the adult actress spoke of being "a boy," not a girl: "she went over the times when, as she said, we were boys together, albeit I had no such penchant for a masculine masquerade as she."[5]

Emma Stebbins took the opportunity while describing Charlotte's youthful tomboyishness to comment on the limitations the concept of femininity placed on little girls like Charlotte:

In those days this epithet, "tomboy," was applied to all little girls who showed the least tendency toward thinking and acting for themselves. It was the advance-guard of that army of opprobrious epithets which has since been lavished so freely upon the pioneers of woman's advancement and for a long time the ugly little phrase had power to keep the dangerous feminine element within what was considered to be the due bounds of propriety and decorum. Things which now any young girl can do as freely as her brother, many of the games which were considered strictly and exclusively masculine, are now open to both sexes alike, to the manifest benefit of the limbs, muscles, and general development of the future mothers of the race.

By how many years of prejudice have had to be slowly undermined and done away before this good could be accomplished, and how much the unwise restraint must have pressed upon this great, strong, free nature, is evidenced by the fact that it is the first thought with which she begins her reminiscences: "I was born a tomboy."[6]

Her tomboyishness, carried over into adult life, became the source of a kind of forbidding power according to William Winter:

Young Charlotte
Cushman. (George
C.D. Odell, *Annals of
the New York Stage.*
Columbia University
Press. Reprinted with
permission.)

She neither employed, nor made pretence of employing, the soft allurements of her sex. She was incarnate power: she dominated by intrinsic authority; she was a woman born to command and to such minds as comprehend authentic leadership she achieved immediate, complete and permanent conquest. . . . You might resent her dominance, and shrink from it, calling it "masculine"; you could not doubt her massive reality nor escape the spell of her imperial power.[7]

Even in an age which saw the production of many breeches parts, Charlotte Cushman's performance of male roles was extraordinary. She continued to "play" the tomboy for the rest of her life. As a stock actress she performed in more than thirty male roles and was regarded as one of the best breeches figures in America. Her Romeo was particularly admired by critics, many of whom believed that she was the best, male or female, that they had ever seen. Others were disgusted with the excessive masculinity of an actress in any breeches part. Observers believed that she completely submerged her femininity in her wooing of Juliet. One London critic, Westland Marsden, reported that

Charlotte and Susan Cushman as Romeo and Juliet. (Library of Congress)

her ardour "exceeded any male actor I have ever seen in the part."[8] Another witness to one of her performances of Romeo reported that "her amorous endearments were of so erotic a character that no man would have dared indulge them *coram publico.*"[9] Her most famous performance as Romeo was in a London cast with her sister as Juliet. Stebbins claimed that Charlotte first assumed male roles only to promote her sister in this and other female roles in the same cast. The truth of the matter is that Charlotte actually showed a propensity for male roles long before her sister went on the stage. C. D. Odell believed that Charlotte's "homely features and lack of feminine charm drove her to masculine characters."[10] Whatever the reasons, one thing that determined her masculine acting style was that early in her career she took as her model, not an actress, but the British actor William Macready. She imitated his movements, his gestures and inflections. Her voice, it was reported, was already, in her late twenties, as deep as his. Furthermore, many observers thought that Charlotte even looked like Macready. Several newspapers at the time printed verses satirizing an imitation that had become unmistakeable to playgoers.

Thus, a homely woman, lacking feminine grace, achieved supremacy in a profession where beauty and womanliness were understood to be essential. It was certainly not by virtue of her looks or her sex that she became an actress of eminence; instead, she triumphed through a combination of other characteristics, chiefly drive, hard work, and talent. Furthermore, she seems to have flaunted her masculine proclivities, opening up to herself the full range of male roles, which were avoided by women unduly concerned about preserving a feminine image.

Even given her masculine propensities and her failure to marry, Cushman was domestic and motherly. She enjoyed entertaining in her home and maintaining a kind of matronly salon expected of many socially prominent women. Moreover she had an extremely maternal nature, vicariously exercised. Her "children" were her nieces and nephews and her professional protegées. The latter group was usually made up of a bevy of admiring young girls, referred to disparagingly by her detractors as Cushman's harem. According to Stebbins, she had a passionate love for the children in the family. "She called herself their 'Big Mamma,' and she would travel any distance to be present at their birth, even on one occasion crossing the ocean for that purpose. It was her great joy to be the first to receive them in her arms, and she had a feeling that this ceremony made them more her own."[11]

The life of Charlotte Cushman forms a significant chapter in the history of exceptional women in the nineteenth-century. She had economic independence, professional agressiveness, and knowledge of a world entirely beyond the understanding of the ordinary woman of her

Poses both onstage and offstage earned Cushman the nickname "Charley de Boots." (Harvard Theatre Collection)

time. Indeed, she competed fiercely, independently, and effectively in a world where men controlled finances and professions.

Charlotte Cushman took to the stage from economic necessity and had to continue with her theatrical career in place of the domestic life of the usual nineteenth-century woman—a life for which she betrayed no small yearning. In this she bore a resemblance to Mary Ann Duff and Fanny Kemble. But there are important differences in Cushman's relationship to the stage. Kemble was a strong woman in many matters, but she, like Mary Ann Duff, was passive in her vocation, falling into the profession because there was nothing else, almost biding her time until something better came along. Cushman was, by contrast, always active, decisive, ambitious. Economics alone stood between Mary Ann Duff and the domestic life she preferred. The barrier between Cushman and the life that women expected in her century was much more fundamental. That barrier comprised her own nature and the attitudes of her time. Thus, at the tender age of twenty, as a young actress in Albany, she could see that the stage would be not only her means of survival and fulfilling her potential, but also a way of sublimating many womanly longings that she would never satisfy in the usual ways.

# CHAPTER 6

# ANNA CORA MOWATT

The career of Anna Cora Mowatt Ritchie (1819-1870), who wrote the play *Fashion* and became an actress at twenty-six, is marked with the same unusual events which can be found in the lives of other nineteenth-century actresses. In spite of the comparative kindness with which the stage treated women, it took an extraordinary woman to follow the theatrical profession and a particularly exceptional character to be successful in it. Anna Cora was born in France in 1819 during her father's residence there as an American businessman. Her girlhood was spent in France and in New York. In her girlhood, the century's view of the theater created a dilemma for her: her upper-class family was very well educated, loved the theater, and attended it often. At home she thrived on the encouragement that she was given by her family to write and produce dramas. Her father, a wealthy and prestigious man, even had a stage built for her on which she and her sisters could produce their dramatic creations. By the age of fourteen, she had had much experience as a young playwright and play doctor, but she had never witnessed a professional production of a drama. The reason for this omission was clerical disapproval of the theater. Anna Cora was so completely under the spell of the family minister, an eloquent spokesman against theater attendance, that she refused to go near a theater during her early teens, a course of action that she explains in her *Autobiography:*

Anna Cora's curls were a youthful, lifelong fashion. (Anna Cora Mowatt, *Autobiography of an Actress*)

121

It never occurred to me to inquire what he really knew of theaters; but I trusted implicitly in his supposed information. I determined that I never would enter such a dreadful place. The thought of the imaginary monsters of evil, which I was certainly to behold, kept me away.[1]

But the minister, the Reverend Eastman, proved no match for Fanny Kemble, who was then taking the country by storm. Fourteen-year-old Anna Cora planned to give in just this once to go to the theater. Having found that it was, after all, not the den of iniquity that the Reverend Eastland had described, she was from that time on always with her family when they went to see plays.

Unlike the fathers of most Victorian ladies who were set to learning only handwork, Anna Cora's father determined that she should be a scholar, encouraging her to master Greek, Latin, French, and history. She would always remember her childhood as an extraordinary idyl. If her childhood was unusual, her young girlhood was bizarre. James Mowatt, a twenty-eight-year-old businessman and lawyer, who courted one of Anna Cora's older sisters, began to court the fourteen-year-old Anna Cora instead and proposed marriage to her a year later. When her father insisted that they postpone their wedding, Mowatt was successful in urging her to elope with him. The occasion was one of many in which Anna Cora pled by proxy for her strong-willed father's understanding and forgiveness, this time by sending her sister to announce the elopement. After she had been married for three days, her father relented and welcomed her back home for a visit.

Her life as a wife was little different from her life as a daughter. The unlikely couple moved into Mowatt's mansion, attended by numerous servants who had long been in his charge. Naturally no household duties were expected of the fifteen-year-old bride. Furthermore, convinced that Anna Cora was still a child, Mowatt postponed any sexual expectations of her. At the same time, he continued, as her father had done, to commit himself to her classical education. So that she could have a confidante and companion, he persuaded one of her younger sisters to live with them. In one way, her childhood was cut short by the premature marriage. In another way, the circumstances left her as a kind of superannuated child, always under the supervision of her husband until his illness, five years later, rendered him an old man before she herself could be a woman. Even in middle age she was physically tiny and dressed like a girl, her hair arranged in childlike ringlets.

For six or seven years after her marriage she amused herself as a child might, occupying herself with home theatricals. Once she returned from a theater-going trip to London with trunks of elaborate costumes and scenery for the staging of one play. As well developed and skillfully performed as these amateur theatricals probably were, the whole endeavor strikes one as an extension of a young girl's playing make-believe. So, despite a bout with consumption, which incapacitated her for a year and would always plague her, scholarship and home theatricals were her whole life until she was twenty-two.

In 1841, her Edenic existence abruptly came to an end. A severe illness cost Mowatt his sight, forcing him to give up his law practice. This alone might not have ruined them had Mowatt not continued his wild speculations in stocks throughout his illness: Anna Cora writes in her autobiography: "He always had a fondness for speculations in land, stocks, etc., which, in the absence of other employment, grew into a fatal poison."[2] During his illness she noticed that on some days he was in an uncharacteristic deep depression; on others he was elated. She realized only later than his radical mood swings corresponded to the rise and fall of his stocks. Eventually James had to tell her that he had lost everything but the house and land. By 1841, when she was twenty-two, he had also lost the Melrose estate. She describes the afternoon when James told her, his child wife, the truth, and she suddenly had to face the awful necessity of growing up.

Misfortune sprinkles ashes on the head of the man, but falls like dew upon the heart of the woman, and brings forth germs of strength of which she herself had no conscious possession.

   That afternoon I walked alone for a long time in the lovely arbor that had been erected for my pleasure. It was a magnificent day in autumn. The grapes were hanging in luxuriant purple clusters above my head. The setting sun could scarcely penetrate their leafy canopy of darkest, richest green. They seemed to typify abundance, peace, prosperity. Eve's "Must I leave thee, paradise?" found its echo in my innermost heart. I sat down in my favorite summer house, and strange thoughts came into my head. At first they were vague and wild, but out of the chaos gradually grew distinctness and order. I thought of my eldest sister Charlotte. Her gift was for miniature painting. When the rude storms of adversity had shipwrecked her husband, she had braved the opposition of her friends, of the world, and converted what had been a mere accomplishment into the means of support for herself and her children.[3]

She determined then that she had to become the family breadwinner, a role that she assumed for the rest of James Mowatt's life. It was difficult at the time to think beyond the resolution. The only two professions open to gentlewomen, sewing and schoolteaching, were ones for which she had no qualifications. She could read Greek but knew nothing of English grammar or grade school mathematics or young children. What she finally decided to do was to turn her child-hood play into a deadly serious endeavor: she would give public readings of American writers and Sir Walter Scott.

As Eric W. Barnes, one of her biographers, pointed out, entering the professional theater at this time was unthinkable: "At the moment she could only regret that the one means she possessed for survival was outlawed by a barrier of opinion which even a mind as ingenious as hers could not surmount."[4] The decision to do readings was a com-promise, made with trepidation. Her sister, weeping copiously, tried to convince Anna Cora that she had taken a self-destructive course. Many of her friends expressed their indignation over her plans, not only snubbing her, but even going so far as to accuse her of besmirching their social class.

The general public was blatantly curious about her appearances in 1841 for several reasons. No one had known a woman of such high social standing with the audacity to make a public spectacle of herself. Nor had anyone ever seen a "female elocutionist." She was the first.

The readings were not the answer to all her problems. She was able to keep the wolf from the door, but not to save Melrose, their family estate that James had lost through speculation. Nor was she physically strong. After a series of readings, she usually collapsed. Although many of her reviews were good, as Barnes points out, much of the press treated her shabbily.

> The wagging tongues would not leave her alone. Some of the newspapers refused to criticize her work at all, devoting themselves to Anna Cora personally. They accused her of setting a precedent which if followed by other women would lead to the dissolution of the home and a general relaxation of moral standards. In an article in *The Ladies Companion* she was denounced in scathing terms. It was bad enough that Mrs. Mowatt should read poetry in public, but that she should do so before mixed audiences seemed nothing less than depravity.[5]

During these financially difficult but artistically promising times, Ed-mund Simpson, manager of the Park, offered her a position as an actress. She turned down the offer immediately, humiliated rather than flattered by it. That she should even be considered for a position as an actress seemed to make all the charges of "depravity" true.

She had to give up the readings almost as soon as she began them. As usual, everything seemed to go wrong at once. Her husband's illness worsened at the same time that her own illness flared up. As a consequence, Anna Cora suffered a nervous collapse. The only thing that quieted the chest pains and coughing was mesmerism. At one time she stayed hypnotized for two weeks, during which time James and her hypnotist took her out riding in a carriage, being careful to secure a veil over her face so that she would not alarm passersby with her forbidding appearance, her eyes rolled back in her head so that only the whites showed. During these trances a second personality began to be released—a laughing, uninhibited gypsy girl, very different from the demure, childlike Anna Cora. She depended on mesmerism for the rest of her life, and she and James, partly from their experiences with its healing powers, became religious Spiritualists.

Even though the treatment rendered her relatively pain-free and calm, she was in no state to resume the grueling chore of public readings. Still, money had to come from somewhere, no matter how ill she was. Her solution this time was to turn to writing. From 1842 until 1845 she supported herself and James by her pen, writing articles of every kind for numerous periodicals, publishing a novel called *The Fortune Hunter,* and turning out volume after volume of practical books on everything from cookery to first aid, many of which appeared under assumed names. She was so successful that James was able to establish his own publishing house, which saw into print her *Life of Goethe* as well as the mountains of manuals and other fiction. At the end of this period, in 1845, she finished the play called *Fashion.* This first successful play written about American manners, with a long run of twenty nights, marked another important turning point in her life. James had declared bankruptcy again when his publishing house failed and at this particularly inopportune time, after completing *Fashion,* she went dry as a writer. The many plays she had planned to write would not be written. She had to turn elsewhere for money.

Only in 1845, when Anna Cora was twenty-six, did the career for which she had been in preparation all her life seem plausible. She had, of course, already broken a considerable barrier by reading in public. Probably more important, during rehearsals for *Fashion* she was afforded an accurate picture of backstage life. She had been interested in what she had seen. It was, she discovered, neither glamorous nor horrible. Other barriers fell away: her husband encouraged the venture and her father approved.

The reputation she had made as a reader-performer and playwright stood her in good stead, for when it was known that she was available as an actress, she immediately received an invitation to play a major role in New York's Park Theater. All the Mowatts' remaining capital and credit went into costumes and coaching. The one thing she was not prepared for was the scorn of veteran actors when she arrived backstage for her first rehearsal. However, by the end of that run-through she received a round of applause from a company that had come to the rehearsal to condemn her as a novice. Her reception by the audience was no less enthusiastic. The *New York Herald* of June 14, 1845, gave her the following review:

> When the curtain fell, the applause was tremendous. A gentleman in the pit called out "three cheers," and three loud cheers were accordingly given, with "one cheer more" in obedience to the request of a fat gentleman in one of the boxes, who, although ready to sink from the heat, contributed more than his share of plaudits. Mrs. Mowatt soon appeared, led on by Mr. Crisp. The cheers—shouts—screams—plaudits—burst forth afresh, whilst a whirlwind of pocket handkerchiefs swept over the boxes, and five or six hundred pairs of boots thundered in the galleries. Mrs. Mowatt curtsied, and a shower of bouquets fell at her feet.

Eric Barnes maintained that there was no other instance of a woman so late in life "starting at the top and maintaining that position through-out her professional life,"[6] a total of eight years.

After Anna Cora made her debut, she pursued her career as if she were in a race that would end tomorrow, traveling all over the country, accepting every offer, taking on any new role in order to keep on working. When other actors of prominence rested in the summer off-season, she committed herself to a rigorous schedule at Niblo's Theater in New York City. She worked harder and for longer hours than she ever had in her life. In her first year as an actress she played two hundred nights in twenty roles. Laurence Hutton wrote of this phe-nomenal woman: "In the annals of the stage of all countries, there is no single instance of a mere novice playing so many times before so many different audiences and winning so much merited praise as did Mrs. Mowatt during the first twelve months of her career as an actress."[7] In 1845, Edgar Allan Poe, expressing the majority opinion of her

Anna Cora Mowatt, playwright. (Library of Congress)

performances, gave her high praise in several long reviews appearing in the *Broadway Journal,* stating that, with the exception of physical force, "she has all the elements of a great actress. . . . Her general grace of manner has never, in our opinion, been equalled on the stage." During the 1845-46 season she played at Niblo's in New York, toured New York State, returned to the Park for engagements, and started off the Chestnut Street Theater's season in Philadelphia. As if her heavy schedule of appearances at urban theaters were not enough, she accepted offers to play the provinces—Charleston, Savannah, New Orleans, and Memphis. The plays she appeared in most frequently between 1845 and 1847 were *The Lady of Lyons, School for Scandal, The Stranger,* and her own *Fashion.* Strangely enough, with all the responsibility, all the physical and mental exertion, her health improved markedly.

In November of 1837 she and James began a London tour. The prospects of a London engagement frightened her because the British had never been cordial to any American actor except Charlotte Cushman. Her fears seemed well founded when her English fellow actors held up English actresses to her as models during rehearsals. However, after one or two performances, Anna Cora's reception was, if not wildly laudatory as it had been in America, at least respectable. Her company drew good crowds in what had otherwise been poor seasons at the Olympic and the Marylebone theaters.

As usual in her life, exceptionally good luck seemed to invite bad. In the middle of the British engagement, James became critically ill. Payment for his treatments during the months before he died required an immense sacrifice on her part: it meant having to leave him and undertake a grueling schedule, much more laborious than she had at first planned. Misfortune begat misfortune: on tour she was suddenly stricken with brain fever and had to be confined to bed miles away from James. When she recovered and was reunited with him in November of 1848, he confessed to her that he had sunk all her earnings into a theatrical scheme that had failed. She recalls in her *Autobiography* the devastating effect that this news had on her:

> Then, for the first time, Mr. Mowatt disclosed to me that by far the larger portion of all we possessed, the hard earnings of a long period of exertion, had for business purposes, been left in the hands of the manager of the Olympic Theater. In his ruin it had been swept away. It became needful that I should resume my labors the instant I felt able. I pass over what this intelligence was to me. Life in all its bitter necessities—its hard requirements—had brought no extremity that tried me as did this.[8]

Brain fever had left her drained, and she was far from recovered. She desperately wanted to remain with her dying husband, but his news forced her to go back on the road prematurely. In February of 1851 she was called back to London: James had died while she was on tour. His only request was that she be strong enough to continue her career in the face of objections by friends and family. She tried to honor his request, and immediately began a series of tours in England. From February until July she played in Newcastle, Leeds, Sheffield, Manchester, and Liverpool before setting sail for America, a widow at the age of thirty-two.

Until 1853 she continued to tour America even though she was ill with an undiagnosed disease. Time after time she was too weak to go on, forcing the cancellation of performances. One wonders why, for two years, she continued to push herself, always sick, always drained of energy. The answer lies at least partially in her Swedenborgian religious beliefs, which held that mind could conquer matter. She clung tenaciously to the idea that if she willed herself to be well, she would be well. Her mind could not, however, conquer the illness, which was finally diagnosed as malaria, and her tour ended. From 1853 until 1854 she recuperated, working on her autobiography, eager to go on tour again as soon as she was able. In 1854 her *Autobiography,* written during this time, was published. Its success is shown in the sale of twenty thousand copies within a year.

In the same year, now thirty-six, she quit the stage and married a wealthy, aristocratic Richmond newspaperman named Foushee Ritchie, who had been pursuing her for two years. It was a disastrous move on her part. In his Richmond home she met with bitter prejudice not only against actors, but against Swedenborgianism as well. Furthermore, she discovered Foushee to be an incurable profligate who made little effort to keep secret his mistresses. She stayed with him for six years, enduring his open scorn of her religion and the hatred of her neighbors, a situation made worse by growing sectional tensions. She waited until 1860, until after the death of her father, before she left Foushee. For awhile, after she had sailed for Europe, seemingly with no notion of ever returning, she kept up a pretense that she was not really separated from Foushee. By the time he came for her in Europe, where she lived with her sister, she had seemingly been able to face the truth of his infidelities and cruelties and was able to tell him exactly why she would never come back to him.

The failure of her marriage left her on her own again financially. She had had a six-year reprieve from financial worry for which she had paid dearly. She no longer had the physical strength to turn to the stage—her first love and her sustenance in times past. Instead, in 1862, she took another route that had earlier proven productive: she returned to writing. In America she supervised the editions of the many books she had previously published, making enough money to enable her to live for a time in Italy and then to spend the rest of her life in London. In these years of declining health, from 1862 until 1870, she worked occasionally as a foreign correspondent, took part in amateur theatricals again, worked as a tutor, and even though bedridden, continued to write. At one point her bad health forced her to refuse a badly needed $50,000 offered in exchange for a professional acting appearance.

Anna Cora's relationship with the theater had dimensions that are not seen in Mary Ann Duff's and Fanny Kemble's. She seemed to love acting. In contrast to Fanny Kemble, Anna found public reading to be a bore once she had been introduced to acting, and she pronounced that she much preferred the latter. Necessity and love joined in her profession, something that James Mowatt certainly understood. She seemed never to have been driven onto the stage. Once she took that first step, she never again hesitated for lack of desire.

Charlotte Cushman embraced her profession in lieu of husband and children, and there is evidence of the same profound psychological drive in Anna Cora's case. Acting compensated for the lack of a normal marriage and for the absence of the children she wanted. She handled physical and emotional frustrations in several ways: through hypnosis, by cultivating Spiritualism, and by acting. In mesmerism she released the gypsy woman within her character who could speak her mind and give way to wild laughter and uninhibited dancing. In Spiritualism, she transcended or sublimated her troublesome flesh. Onstage, she threw her energy into hard physical work, giving vent to a range of emotions. The stage was Anna Cora's miracle: in the theater that fragile and sickly frame took on strength and endurance; the old nervous disorders gave way to a kind of grace.

Anna Cora was a woman without a home as surely as was Mary Ann Duff; that is, she had no sphere in which she truly belonged. Her father's house and that lost Melrose of her late teens were the last homes she was to know. After she entered the stage, she would never find a home within the class into which she had been born. She had betrayed her social class by forming an alliance with the theater. Even though she had all her life prepared herself for the stage and loved acting, she was something of an outsider, a neophyte, a usurper in the eyes of veteran performers. She was not of their class either; she shared neither their manners nor their experiences. She was often under suspicion because, many assumed, she came from the upper class as a missionary, intent on reform.

Her second marriage brought her a place of residence but no home. Richmond, like the theater and her own social class, was hostile, resentful of her presence. What makes her situation so puzzling is that the hostility seems entirely unmerited, for she was an honest, gentle, and considerate person of unimpeachable character. But unlike Mary Ann Duff, who yearned so plaintively for a home, Anna Cora braved her sudden, unmerited, and perpetual homelessness with little complaint or regret. She was sustained instead by the belief that she had known a soul-mate in her husband James, by her devotion to her religion, and her conviction that she had discovered and practiced her true vocation.

*Anna Cora Mowatt*

Anna Cora Mowatt met many trials with great poise and few complaints. (Library of Congress)

# CHAPTER 7

# LAURA KEENE

Little is known about the life of one of the most influential figures of the nineteenth-century stage—a woman named Laura Keene (1824-1873). The sources are few, and the information inadequate and inaccurate. An 1897 biography by John Creahan, who knew the actress personally, is a strange hodgepodge of such things as a defense of Roman Catholicism and a large collection of irrelevent letters written by Laura Keene's daughter. Furthermore, he seems to have deliberately misrepresented facts in order to turn the scandalous Laura into a Victorian lady. A newspaper column and a letter, both of which appeared in the *New York Dramatic Mirror,* can be used to correct some of Creahan's fabrications, and information about her professional life is amply available in stage histories and in memoirs written by actors who worked for her. A biographical sketch by Joseph Donahue is not very useful.

Since a reliable and comprehensive biography is lacking, separating fact from legend regarding Laura Keene's early London years is a difficult task. Creahan, for example, gives her birthdate as 1826. Odell gives it as 1820. Creahan writes that Keene went to work as an actress right after her father died, when she was fifteen years old. Sources in the *Dramatic Mirror* insisted that her first job when a young girl in her teens was not acting but tending bar in a tavern on Hungerford Stairs, where she was known as "Red Laura"

Laura Keene appeared deceptively fragile and demure. (Harvard Theatre Collection)

133

because of her auburn hair. Creahan suggested that she was often in the company of artists as a child and knew William Turner personally. Other accounts reveal an early family association with actors: an uncle who was a comedian and an aunt who supposedly taught Laura something about acting.

Laura was probably fifteen or sixteen when she married a man named John Taylor. According to Creahan, Taylor was a member of the nobility. Other sources, however, agree that he was a former soldier who had left the army to set up business for himself as a pub owner. One writer contended that she was tricked into marriage with Taylor. Supposedly after the two were married, they ran the pub together and eventually had two daughters. They parted ways, however, before Laura reached the age of twenty. Creahan related only one reason for the failure of the marriage—John Taylor's indolence. From all other accounts, Creahan left out a few details: after their pub failed (a pub, by the way, that Creahan conveniently overlooked), Taylor was arrested for a serious crime and was banished for life to a foreign prison. Laura seems to have been under the impression that his arrest, conviction, and deportation constituted a divorce. It was only then that she began seriously cultivating associates in the London theaters. She also began having an affair with a wealthy man named Lyster-Kaye, whom the *Dramatic Mirror* identifies as her only real love. The anonymous author of one letter claims that she wore Lyster-Kaye's monogram in diamonds around her neck for the rest of her life. Finally, through the help of a friend, she received an acting position in the company of the fabulous Madame Vestris.

It was a prophetic beginning for Laura Keene's career that she should be hired by the first great female manageress of the nineteenth-century. In Vestris's theater Laura could observe this rare instance of a successful businesswoman. Here was a model for the young girl to follow, proof that a woman could reasonably aspire to a place of prominence in a profession. Vestris was in a position to make all the decisions in her company, to supervise an artistic creation, and she was a financial success as well. Laura later even adopted something of Vestris's style. Although she never went so far as to take on her first employer's habit of slapping the faces of actors who disappointed her, Laura was, like Madame Vestris, a tyrannical, often cruel, manager. While playing in Vestris's London company, she was noticed by J. W. Wallack, manager of one of New York's most successful theaters, and at his invitation she left for America with her mother and two daughters to begin a career that took her to all parts of the United States, the country that she adopted for the rest of her life.

Her ambition as well as a degree of unscrupulous opportunism were apparent from the beginning of her American career. When she came to Wallack's theater she was probably about twenty. She immediately became a favorite with the public in New York, but the urge for greater things caused her to desert Wallack on very short notice. In his memoirs Wallack's son, Lester, gave a bitter account of Laura's breach of agreement, a particularly embarrassing incident for him because it occurred while the elder Wallack was absent from town on business, leaving Lester with the awesome responsibility of running the company. On one night, when the curtain was due to go up on *The Rivals,* Laura Keene was nowhere to be found. Curtain time was delayed and panic broke out backstage as the audience, becoming dangerously restless, answered the repeated apologies of the younger Wallack by stomping

Keene's elaborate New York theatre.  (Library of Congress)

and yelling for their favorite: "Keene! Keene!" Laura never did appear, and further investigation revealed that she was not likely to. With no warning whatsoever, she had packed up and moved to Baltimore, accompanied by a man identified as John Lutz. Lester Wallack, understandably incensed, was forced to inform an angry audience, who had paid good money to see Red Laura, that she would not appear. In the next few days she sent a concocted story to the newspapers to explain her unwarranted exit; without a modicum of shame, she claimed that she had left town to nurse a sick brother.

With her move to Baltimore, John Lutz, a well-known, sometimes successful professional gambler, began, by all accounts, to live with her and take some part in managing her career. When he had the funds, he financed her tours and experiments in management, as he now did in Baltimore; but he was more often low on funds because of the uncertain nature of his business and his love of high living. At such times, he depended on the income from her talents. Almost every biographical source offers a different version of Keene's relationship with Lutz, and it is virtually impossible to ferret out the truth. Two different stories appear in the *Dramatic Mirror*. One of them states that she married Lutz at about the time she left Wallack's and moved to Baltimore, being under the misapprehension that she was automatically divorced from her first husband at the time of his imprisonment. Creahan stated that Laura and Lutz were not married until 1860, when she discovered that her first husband was dead. Whether or not she ever married Lutz, her relationship with him was a long-standing one, lasting from her appearance in New York until his death.

The anonymous author of "The Romance of Laura Keene" in the *Dramatic Mirror* contended that Laura embarked on her venture to the western United States after rumors reached her that her first husband was alive and in California. She may have wanted to find out the truth of the rumors and determine the status of her marriage. She did not find Taylor in California, but while she was working there, Mrs. Sarah Kirby-Stark, a California actress and manager who had recently returned from a foreign tour, supposedly informed Laura that she had found Taylor serving a life prison sentence in Australia. On the strength of this information, Laura secretly boarded a ship carrying Edwin Booth and a company of other actors to Australia. Why Laura pledged the captain of the vessel to secrecy and boarded quietly in the middle of the night remains a mystery. Once they had left port, she appeared openly and let it be known to the actors that she would like to join Booth's company on its Australian tour. She appeared with them in a few productions, but their schedule soon interfered with her own plans to search for Taylor, so she struck out on her own to play more remote areas where she would have a better chance of locating him.

Eventually she found him, serving a life sentence on an Australian chain gang. After talking with Taylor, she rejoined Booth's company briefly and then left for California by way of Hawaii.

Even if this story is true, no hint is given of what she was able to establish in her meeting, but the carefully kept secret of Taylor's existence was already in sufficient circulation to cause a scandal when she returned to the United States. Only after the Australian trip was it somehow apparent to the general public that the girls whom she had been calling her nieces were really her daughters. Rumors circulated accusing her of bigamy and of deceiving the public about her daughters because, it was charged, they were illegitimate. Even though what she wanted to determine by the long trip to Australia is a puzzle and what she decided about her marriage on the basis of what she found is a mystery, she satisfied herself, supposedly, that Taylor was still alive and married to her. She still probably made no move to divorce him, for it is unlikely that a legitimate marriage to Lutz, if it ever took place at all, occurred before Taylor died in 1860. Since she had been living with Lutz for so many years before this, the assumption is that she would have married him had there been no legal barrier.

Creahan believes that Laura's refusal to divorce Taylor can be attributed to her staunch Roman Catholicism. One of the *Dramatic Mirror* stories contends that she never wanted to marry Lutz but was terrorized into remaining with him. In any case, the public's discovery of her daughters and the open alliance with Lutz branded her as scandalous in the eyes of many people even in the theatrical community. William Winter, for example, was extremely reluctant to recognize her contributions to the American theater and insisted that an unstable character kept her from being the great actress and manageress that she could have been.

These early scandals, which came to light after Keene's Australian tour, followed her across the country to New York. When her career as a manager began in New York City in 1855, it was shadowed by disgrace. Laura's unsavory personal reputation was soon the least of her worries, however. A strong group of antagonistic managers was determined that this upstart female would fail in all attempts to compete

Laura Keene fought
the New York
establishment.
(George C. D. Odell,
*Annals of the New York
Stage,* Columbia
University Press.
Reprinted with
permission.)

with the theatrical establishment of the city. Yet Keene seems to have
regarded her wars with rival managers as no more than temporary
irritations as she launched what became one of the most successful
managerial careers on the American stage. Wherever she worked, she
made stage history—whether it was in the highly successful Laura
Keene Theatre or on the tours for which she was so famous.

Many of the actors who performed with her company left accounts
of her particular way of running a theater. Most of them emphasize

two characteristics: her ingenuity in handling a variety of jobs necessary in putting on a production and her shrewd business sense. She was not above working in any capacity in her business. Her abilities certainly went beyond acting and design to include every humble aspect of stagecraft. As Creahan wrote, "in the mechanical department of a theater, whether in the cellar or in the 'flies,' she seemed equally at home."[1] The testimony given Creahan by an actress in Laura's company is typical of the accounts left by those who worked for her:

> Laura Keene could take a piece of paste-board, a pencil and calipers, and in an hour's time furnish drawings of stage settings or scenes for new plays for her stage manager, scene painter and head carpenter, such as could not be conceived or thought of by any other actor or actress in the business.[2]

The most mind-boggling anecdote to illustrate the extent of Keene's nerve and ingenuity was recorded by Kate Reignolds in *Yesterday with Actors:*

> One night, when *Much Ado about Nothing* was to be given, it was found almost at the last moment that the costumes were not ready. All the women not in the cast were instantly pressed into service. Under Laura Keene's direction, the unfinished garments were sewn upon the wearers. The time running short, the distracted manager, who had her own hands full, and was still to dress for "Beatrice," called the lords and attendants to stand before her, and sending to the paint room for a pot and brush, finished the borders of their "jackets and trunks" in black paint! "Now, keep apart! Don't sit down! Don't come near the ladies!" with her spasmodic, quick speech, and she was off to array herself in a twinkling, for the dainty lady of Messina![3]

Her business acumen as actress and manager was legend. For example, Louisa Eldredge, an actress who worked with her, recounted a time when Keene refused to allow the curtain to go up until the owner of the theater had paid her. When he saw that she would not go on without the money, a man from the box office was sent backstage to deliver her a roll of bills which, Louisa Eldredge says, "she quietly counted, placed in her bosom," before telling the prompter to ring up the curtain. After the show, the company discovered that the theater owner would not have paid them otherwise.

Both audiences and theatrical reviewers regarded her as a superb showperson and manager. A *New York Sun* review of January 12, 1862, illustrates the kind of praise she regularly received:

Of all the theaters, both for manager and plays, commend me to Laura Keene's. The fair Laura, herself an unexcelled actress, and excellent judge of artists and plays, holds ready a friendly hand both for home and foreign productions, provided they be good. This is the theater for all our citizens, and this is the reason for the great success of the *American Cousin,* a piece made more popular at Miss Keene's theater than any theatrical production ever yet presented at any theater in the world.[4]

Those who worked for her agreed that she was a hard, exacting, and sometimes unjust master. William Winter reported that she "looked like an angel, but was, in fact, a martinet," that she ruled her company "with imperious, sometimes even arrogant authority," and was "self-willed, volatile, capricious and imperious."[5] His judgment was largely substantiated by Reignolds and Jefferson. Odell reported that Laura was not incapable of attacking other managers in the press and stealing talent from other companies. Although Joseph Jefferson insisted that he and Laura Keene were on friendly terms after he left her company, the record of his work with her is made up of accounts of their disagreements. She was, according to this amiable actor, frequently short tempered, jealous of her position, suspicious of her stars, and often foolish in her choice of plays.

Nevertheless, her theater flourished during the Civil War, when others were folding or playing to empty houses. Finally she abandoned her management of a permanent theater in New York in order to go on tour again. George C. D. Odell believed that this change was necessitated by a flagging career, but as Creahan pointed out, it was not unusual for stars as eminent as Booth and Jefferson to begin touring at the height of their success because being on the road was often more financially and artistically rewarding than staying in one place. It is true that Laura always loved a change of scenery and sought out opportunities to tour throughout her career.

It was in 1865, not long after she had abandoned her New York theater, that she experienced the greatest trauma of her life. Her highest moment of tragedy was not a stage role but a test of her mettle as a real human being. In 1865 she had taken her company to Ford's Theatre in Washington, D. C. where she planned a performance of her now famous *Our American Cousin.* Her heroism on that night of Lincoln's appearance at the theater draws no attention now and drew no appreciation then, but in her actions following the shooting we have proof of her amazing strength of character. On the evening of the president's

Keene as a figure in a tragedy. (Library of Congress)

appearance, Laura Keene was in the wings, waiting for her entrance cue, when John Wilkes Booth, who was not in the cast, rushed from the stage carrying a dagger and struck her hand out of his way as he ran by. Immediately she heard an outcry from the audience—some of the voices called, "Kill the actors!" When in the confusion she learned that Lincoln had been shot, she rushed onstage and managed to quiet an audience that had become a panic-stricken mob, venting some of its rage against the actors in the play. She then proceeded up to Lincoln's box just as an hysterical Mary Todd Lincoln was being escorted away. Laura rushed to the president and held his head in her lap until men arrived to take him to the house across the street. Seaton Monroe, a reporter for the *North American Review,* gave the following account of her on that day in April 1865. He had arrived in the theater just as Lincoln was being carried from the box:

> Attired as I had so often seen her, in the costume of her part in *Our American Cousin,* her hair and dress were in disorder, and not only was her gown soaked in Lincoln's blood, but even her cheeks where her fingers had strayed, were bedaubed with the sorry stains! But lately the central figure in the scene of comedy, she now appeared the incarnation of tragedy.[6]

Keene's involvement in this national tragedy did not end in Ford's Theatre. She was the first witness to identify the assassin as John Wilkes Booth, an actor with whom the whole company was acquainted. Despite her willingness to assist the authorities, she and the entire company, including the owner of the theater, Ford, were tainted with the suspicion of conspiracy with Booth. During the weekend following the assassination, she and her troupe decided to continue their tour, but their train was stopped near Harrisburg, Pennsylvania, where they were arrested by the Secret Service. They were held until John Lutz, who had connections in high places, rushed to the War Office to use his influence in securing their release. After a few days they were allowed to continue, but others of the company who remained in Washington were arrested and forced to report daily to the authorities. The motivation for Keene's arrest was incomprehensible: witnesses had seen Booth strike her when she blocked his way in the wings of the theater, and she had not hesitated to identify him when others had been reluctant to involve themselves. One student of the events surrounding the death of Lincoln, Theodore Roscoe, speculated that "Stanton probably ordered her arrest as a sop to public opinion."[7]

Keene at the height of
her managerial career.
(George C.D. Odell,
*Annals of the New York
Stage*. Columbia
University Press.
Reprinted with
permission.)

In any event, that bloody night, her subsequent role in identifying
Booth, the humiliating arrest in Pennsylvania, and the suspicions that
continued to surround her all took their toll on what was already a
fragile physical nature. Her reputation suffered irreparable damage.
Odell believed that she was never able to recover, emotionally or
professionally. It is a fact that her health and her career went downhill
from the time of this event.

Keene was engaged for the rest of her life in a series of projects
designed to recoup her career and her fortune. John Lutz, who had
been her companion since about 1852, died five years after Lincoln's

*Lenra Keene*

This pose catches
something of the
seductive "Red Laura"
of London fame.
(Library of Congress)

assassination, having spent all of their money in maintaining a luxurious
lifestyle. She was emotionally spent and penniless. To pay his debts,
she joined another woman in the publication of a periodical called *The
Fine Arts*. One speculation about why she began this ill-advised project
with such determination is that she needed another source of income.
Life on the stage had become too rigorous for her delicate health. As

her friends said it would, the periodical folded within a year. The need for a different source of income also may have prompted the lecture tour that she undertook in 1872. In addition, she managed to put together an acting company and find occasional roles for herself until failing health caused her to withdraw in the summer of 1873. On November 4, 1873, she died of consumption at the age of forty-seven. Stories vary about her financial situation in these last days. Although Creahan claimed that she was still able to live comfortably to the end and leave her daughters an estate sufficient to support them for the rest of their lives, it is generally believed that she died in poverty.

Keene's life was like that of a Victorian man's—always dictated by work. She was a responsible provider and not a typical mother. She never allowed her family life to interfere with her career, her frequent tours, her constant changes of location, and her long and peculiar work schedule. She did not have, and did not seem to want, the domestic life of other Victorian women. She never settled in one place for very long; she was never confined to the hearth or devoted to performing household chores for a husband or her two children. Her mother who lived with her from the time Laura came to America until she died in the 1860s, was the "mother" of Laura's daughters for all intents and purposes and was even called "Mother" by the girls. For all of Laura's life, her daughters continued the early habit, calling their real mother, "Aunt Laura."

Unlike Fanny Kemble, Mary Ann Duff, and Anna Cora Mowatt, Laura Keene entered the stage as a young girl, seemingly more from a personal attraction to the profession than from the need for money alone. It might be argued that Charlotte Cushman and Adah Menken also loved the stage as Kemble and Duff did not, but not even these two ambitious women were so thoroughly professional as was Laura Keene. She was not just a star; she was not just an actress. She was a master of almost every aspect of theatrical life, and it all came to her as naturally as breathing. For no other actress in this volume was the stage so all sufficient. Cushman gloried in high society, and Menken craved her literary association, but the be-all and end-all of Laura Keene's life was the theater.

# _Chapter 8_

# ADAH ISAACS MENKEN

Adah Isaacs Menken (1835-1869) was one of the prominent actresses of the nineteenth century who reinforced the stereotype of the actress as wildly unconventional in her private life. She was more interesting as a personality and a star than she was skillful as an actress, but she had a decided impact on the image of the profession in the mind of the century.

Nineteenth-century accounts of her origins are confusing and incomplete because she wanted to remain enigmatic, not from shame or bashfulness, but because she knew the value of mystery in perpetuating public interest. She knew that mystery was the raw material of legend, and she was successful in becoming the legend that she set out to be. The different names she is assumed to have had and the conflicting stories of her background before she entered the stage would fill a volume. She cultivated the myth that her mother was a Parisian and that her parents were wealthy enough to take her on frequent European trips as a child. Another persistent myth was that she was a student of the classics who had read Greek and Latin as a child. The truth seems to be that she was born in Milne, Louisiana, of humble parents whose names remained a mystery even to those who knew her intimately. As a young teenager, when her stepfather died, she supported her mother and sister by tutoring and, according to biographer Alan Lesser, by dancing on the stage in New Orleans.[1]

Menken risked life and limb for fame in the role of Mazeppa. (Harvard Theatre Collection)

147

No detail of Menken's early life can be accepted without question. Supposedly she lived for a time in Havana, Cuba, and later conned her family and friends—even perhaps herself—into believing that she had been a stage star there. Some accounts indicate that she had a thriving stage career in New Orleans in her late teens. On the other hand, Noel Gerson contended that she did not actually get onstage until after her marriage. While she was searching for stage roles, she met and married, in 1856, Alexander Isaacs Menken, a Jewish businessman. He took her to his home in Cincinnati, where she seemed to enjoy the life of a housewife and poet. Her husband, however, tired of his father's business, and, believing that Adah had been a star, made plans to exploit her talent. He managed to get her some roles on tour and eventually a starring role in New Orleans. Her ability at this time to talk herself into stardom is illustrated by a story told by James Murdock, a Shakespearian actor of some prominence:

I was fulfilling a short engagement in Nashville, Tenn., and the manager had made an arrangement with Miss Adah Isaacs Menken (so famous for her Mazeppa performances) to act the leading female characters in my plays. I found her, however, to be a mere novice, and not at all qualified for the important situation to which she had aspired. But she was anxious to improve and willing to be taught. A woman of personal attractions, she made herself a great favorite in Nashville. She dashed at everything in tragedy and comedy with a reckless disregard of consequences, until at length, with some degree of trepidation, she paused before the character of Lady Macbeth! I found in the first rehearsal that she had no knowledge of the part save what she had gained from seeing it performed by popular actresses of the day. . . .

So she came to me and frankly said, "I know nothing of this part, and have a profound dread of it, but I must act it, for I have told the manager that I was up to the performance of all the leading characters." . . . I accordingly gave the lady a few general ideas of the action of the part, and finished by begging her at least to learn the *words*, and for the acting trust to chance. Night came, and with it came Miss Menken arrayed to personate the would-be queen. She grasped the letter and read it in the approved style, holding it at arms' length and gaspingly devouring the words with all the intensity of ferocious desire; then, throwing her arms wildly over her head, she poured out such an apostrophe to guilt, demons, and her own dark purposes that it would have puzzled any one acquainted with the text to guess from what unlimited "variorum" she could have studied the part. However, as Casca said of Cicero, "He speaks Greek!" and Miss Menken spoke what the people thought was "Shakespeare," and, for aught they knew to the contrary, it might have been Greek too.

Flushed with her reception and the lavish applause which followed the reading of the letter, she entered on the next scene, where Lady Macbeth chastises the flagging will of her consort "with the valor of her tongue," and at her sneering reference to "the poor cat i' the adage" she swept by her liege lord as if he were a fit object for derision and contempt; and they came another round of applause. After Macbeth's announcement that he was capable of doing "all that dare become a man," the lady returned to the charge with most determined scorn and denunciation, and in tones which might have become a Xantippe. . . . Here, "taking the stage," she rushed back to Macbeth, and laying her head on his shoulder whispered in his ear, "I don't know the rest." From that point Macbeth ceased to be the guilty thane, and became a mere prompter in a Scotch kilt and tartans. For the rest of the scene I gave the lady the words. Clinging to my side in a manner very different from her former scornful bearing, she took them line by line before she uttered them, still, however, receiving vociferous applause.[2]

Her husband Alexander, who had encouraged his wife to dress flamboyantly and at whose insistence her stage career had resumed, became angry at the attention she received from other men now that she was an actress. Once she had a taste of theatrical life, however, her ambition was renewed, and she refused to relinquish her career.

The natural step from her New Orleans success and her provincial tours was to move to New York. By the time that Adah took up residence in New York, she and Menken had agreed to part ways. She resented his drinking and his refusal to try to support her. He, on the other hand, resented her success and her immodesty in showing her legs when she played male roles. While she was in New York, Menken obtained a rabbinical divorce from her when she was twenty-three years old. Despite the fact that she had been married for less than two years to Menken and would be married several times thereafter, she chose to keep his name for the rest of her life.

New theater engagements and a new courtship and marriage to boxer John C. Heenan began in the city, along with a new series of troubles. Almost immediately after the wedding, while Heenan was in Europe engaged in a championship match, the roof caved in. Adah's first husband, Alexander Menken, upon hearing of her new alliance, let it be known in a public letter that his divorce, contrary to what Adah had been led to believe, was religious only, that legally Alexander and Adah were still man and wife when she married Heenan. Hence she was a bigamist, and the child she carried was a bastard. Heenan, who had freely received money from her while her career was going well, turned against her and became defensive and stingy, now that their positions were reversed and he was world champion. In a letter published in the *New York Herald* on November 1, 1859, he withdrew his affection, his name, and his support and claimed that he owed her nothing, even though she was carrying his child: "I declare that I was never married to her or to anyone else. I was never possessed of any of her means, and never, to my knowledge, received or spent a dollar of her money."

From that time on, she carried the name of adulteress, even while Augustin Daly and others who had come to know her defended both her motives and her talent. She tried in her own public letter to defend herself against the charges of her first and second husbands: "Heenan may call me an 'adventuress.' He has been nourished by, and subsisted upon, the fruits of my professional labor, until I would no longer furnish supplies for his bacchanalian career, and such an appellation comes from him with a very bad grace."[3]

Sick, penniless, and pregnant, she had to continue working. This was probably the only time in her life when she felt an aversion to her profession. The press continued to make news of her misfortune and she was able to get only a few undesirable engagements with companies of low repute. The career limitations imposed upon women became painfully obvious to her. She thought that she was qualified to teach or to write, but journalism, too, was closed to women; and school teaching was out of the question for a woman of her reputation. Nevertheless, she persisted in keeping up her spirits and determination: "But withal I can work. I hate idleness. But I can only write for papers or book, or teach in a school. I cannot sew or work as many women. I could read or lecture in public, at least I could do something, and I intend to."[4]

Just as Catherine Sinclair had used Edwin Forrest's name to get on the stage after their divorce, so Adah now used the name of Heenan, the boxing champion, to get herself jobs. He was much more in the news than she was after his fight, and she could gain publicity by advertising herself as his wife. Notoriety notwithstanding, she became a big success at the Bowery in *The Protean Comedy*. In April of that year her child was born dead or else it died shortly thereafter. The birth renewed public outrage at her inadvertant bigamy. Neither Heenan nor the public was willing to forgive her carrying an illegitimate child. The press took renewed interest in castigating her, egged on by Heenan's public condemnation of her as a prostitute. As a result, engagements were not forthcoming after the child was born. Despised, penniless, and left in despair, she contemplated suicide.

The Adah who emerged from this dark trial decided to live a different life. It is almost as if, having perceived all too clearly how the world insisted on seeing her and treating her, she now chose to embrace the defiant image and make the most of it. Having tried to recognize the social niceties before, she would now care for them not at all. She began doing precisely what she wanted to do—and society could go to the devil. She was one of the first women in America to cut her hair short; she attended political rallies alone; and she wrote newspaper stories, one called "Women of the World," in which she urged women to train themselves to be self-supporting.

Her luck improved, and she was successful in getting acting jobs, usually in light comedy or spectacles. Having already paid the price, she now reaped the rewards. Theater managers, who had scorned and neglected her before, now sought to capitalize on her notoriety. She played to good houses in Maine, Michigan, Illinois, and New York state. Using the infamous and flamboyant Lola Montez as a model, she developed an aggressive, open, lively style of acting. Henry P. Phelps, in his 1889 memoirs of the Albany stage, wrote sympathetically of the Adah who played in that provincial theater:

> In spite of all that was said about her, she behaved, during this time, like a perfect lady, and won all the hearts by her affectionate manners. . . . The wagging tongues ever ready to assail a woman, and particularly ready if that woman is an actress, have done their work in Europe and America, and in many minds the name of The Menken is a synonym of all that is depraved in the female sex. Those who knew her best, are best aware how unjust was this estimate.[5]

It was while she was appearing in Albany that she was made an offer that would change her career and revolutionize the popular stage: actor James Murdock proposed that she play in *Mazeppa,* an action-filled drama based on the poem by Byron, a writer whom she was said to resemble physically. The role eventually made her famous all over the world. At the time she first developed the part, the perils involved in playing it had even frightened away most male actors from trying it. The most demanding and memorable scene in the play occurs when Mazeppa, a prince who has been stripped of his clothes, is tied to a wild horse, which rears and gallops up a steep ledge, eighteen inches wide, to the top of the theater. As often as not, a dummy had been

This widely distributed photograph of Adah with Dumas meant the end of their affair.
(Harvard Theatre Collection)

used in this scene. Constance Rourke referred to the play as "that abortive circus performance, descended from the poetry of Byron."[6] However, with her usual keen sense of the extraordinary possibilities of any role, Adah insisted on dispensing with the dummy and having herself tied to the back of the horse. Enthusiastic crowds for the next four years came to see her: Adah playing the part in flesh-colored tights and almost killing herself every night on the wild horse. A first-hand account of the initial rehearsals and performances written for the *Albany*

*Mirror,* October 25 1879, by John B. Smith, who ran the Green Street Theater, was recounted by H. P. Phelps in his history of the Albany theater:

> At length, trembling with apprehension, she was placed on the animal's back, but begged, that instead of starting from the footlights, the horse be led up to the run. I humored her in this, and there's where I made a mistake. The horse, thrown out of her usual routine, only went part way up and then, with a terrific crash, plunged off the planking down into the "wreck," as we call it, upon the staging and timbers. My heart was in my mouth, for not only was there the danger that the woman was killed, but that my $200 mare—excuse me, my present, "Belle Beauty"—was ruined forever. First, of course, we lifted out the Menken, pale as a ghost, almost lifeless, and the blood streaming from a wound in her beautiful shoulder. Then with the tackling we had about the theater, we raised up Belle Beauty, and I began picking the slivers out of her. It was a bad business. Miss Menken was found to be not seriously injured, but the doctor said she could not appear on Monday evening. "All the same, the play will be done," said I. "Every dollar I have in the world, and all I can borrow, is in it." Menken roused at this. "I must go on with the rehearsal," said she. This startled me. That she should have the grit to repeat the act, after such an accident, was astounding.[7]

Even during the Civil War when theater was almost dead Adah was touring in *Mezeppa* and other spectacles and playing to packed houses.

In 1862, at the height of her success in New York, she married once more. Her new husband was R. H. Newell, a satirist who wrote under the name of Orpheus C. Kerr. He confessed in his autobiography that he had married her to reform her, a message he did not convey to her. After three days of marriage he unexpectedly insisted that she renounce acting. When she resisted, he even, according to rumor, went so far as to manhandle her and lock her in the house. She jumped out a window and back into a career that took her on a tour of the West. Newell went west for a brief reunion with her but finally returned to New York, leaving her in California.

If her failed marriage caused her any grief, her booming career was a consolation. Her aggressive and cunning business deals caused the money to flow in. Just one example: in 1863 at Tom Macguire's theater in California, where Macguire claimed that half of San Francisco had come to see Adah in her two-and-one-half-week run, she got one-third of the nightly gross—a total of $9,000 for sixteen nights. As a result

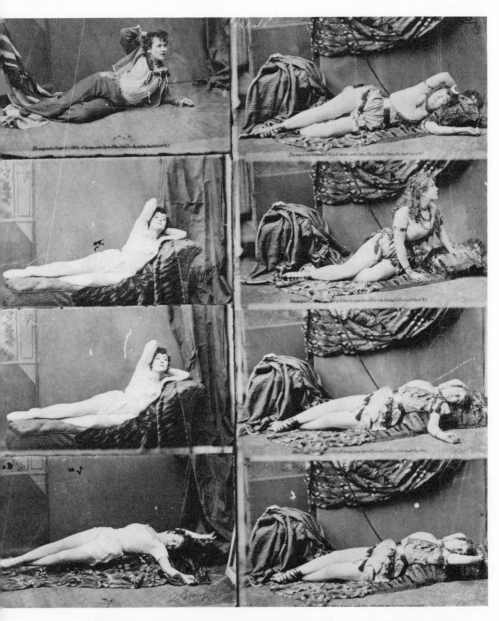

Photographer Sarony caught Adah Menken's ability to project the sexuality that attracted audiences and lovers. (Library of Congress)

of her fantastic success with *Mazeppa,* she was soon adding other horse dramas to her repertoire and even training her own animals.

Throughout Menken's career, her appearances were either in plays of very low quality or in entertainments that could in no way be classified as drama. The *Protean Comedy* entertainment, an evening of poses of different historical characters, was one of her specialties. Her beauty and grace, her good sense of timing and mimicry, guaranteed her success in these "changes," as they were called. She also did burlesques and impersonations of such people as Charlotte Cushman, Edwin Forrest, and Edwin Booth. Good taste rarely was a hindrance. She did not hesitate to burlesque Lola Montez just after the death of that unfortunate woman. Another of Menken's specialties comprised plays in which she could assume more than one character. In *Black-Eyed Susan* she played four characters; in *The French Spy* she played three; in *A Day in Paris,* five. Most of these parts were male characters. And then there was always the ever successful *Mazeppa* and other spin-off horse dramas like *Rookwood.* She would introduce anything that was guaranteed to draw publicity and a big house, anything that would put her in the spotlight for the evening, anything that had a new twist to it, was scandalous or timely. By the mid-sixties, all this had made her the highest paid actress of her day.

She had come to believe that her bad reputation gave her ultimate freedom. If people were going to believe the worst of her anyway, why not make the most of it? She had nothing to lose. So in New York and California she cultivated bohemians for the sheer excitement. In the West she dressed like a man and entered notorious and forbidden gambling dens where she won as much as $2,000 an evening. Betting at the racetrack was another of her unladylike amusements.

She was not disappointed in her reception in England and on the Continent. As she had courted the literary world of Walt Whitman in New York and Bret Harte in California, she now turned her attentions to the writers of London—Dante Gabriel Rossetti, Charles Dickens, Charles Reade, Wilkie Collins—and other English writers who were thoroughly engaged by her wit and beauty and readily entertained her. With her continued popularity, however, she had to weather severe condemnation. The public suspected her of sleeping with every prominent rake in England, a charge that may not have been far from the truth, according to Noel Gerson. In 1866 she met a man named James Paul Barkeley. Her infatuation with him was undoubtedly encouraged by her belief that he was a wealthy speculator in mining stock. By the time that one of her friends informed her that he was a penniless gambler, she was pregnant by him, and she decided to go through a marriage ceremony only to give the child legitimacy. She and Barkeley did not live together after marriage.

After the birth of her son, she took Paris by storm. She was an instant sensation. One of her performances was even graced by Napoleon III. As if this were not enough, house receipts were quadrupled as the result of a stage accident. During one of her appearances, her horse fell, knocking her unconscious for an entire night. Despite broken fingers, bruises, and cuts, she was back on the stage in two days, appearing for thirteen curtain calls. For two months afterward, the lines were long and enthusiastic outside her theater.

In December of 1866 she met the elderly Alexander Dumas, who, at sixty-five, had seen better days. Adah began having an affair with him and provided him with large amounts of money, to the displeasure of his children and friends. The alliance ended after a few months in a highly publicized international scandal, when photographs of the two in an affectionate embrace were copied and sold by the hundreds. At the same time pornographic fakes sold equally well. When the pictures appeared, Dumas's family succeeded in cooling down the affair, but the two apparently kept in touch with one another until Adah died.

In 1867-68, the last year of her life, everything seemed to fall apart. Even the fat profits from her performances were not enough to support her in the style she had come to enjoy, and according to Gerson she began accepting expensive gifts for her sexual favors. When the tolerant Parisian bohemians began to ostracize her, she found it convenient to arrange an extended London engagement. In October of 1867, while playing there, she met Algernon Swinburne and formed her most notorious alliance. Legend has it that her meeting with the poet occurred as the result of a wager; she made a bet with Rossetti that she could get herself into Swinburne's bed, a feat that seemed not only difficult but downright illogical and futile, for he was reported to be both impotent and masochistic. As the story goes, she merely knocked on Swinburne's door in the middle of the night and introduced herself. Supposedly she moved in with him that very night. They regarded each other as soul mates. She was Swinburne's Dolores. He was her male counterpart, the inspiration of poems included in her collection called *Infelicia*. Unfortunately, Adah the poet was not the unqualified success that Adah the stage entertainer had been. When Swinburne dared to criticize her verse, wrote Gerson, she broke off the affair. Another story, told by Allen Lesser and reported in biographies of Swinburne, is that photography again proved her downfall. After several pictures of Adah and Swinburne were made public, his family pressured him to desert her. Some reports indicate that she went into a state of depression because he left her. Others contend that she was relieved to get rid of him, refusing to collect money on her wager and flippantly declaring that Swinburne never learned that love-making involved more than biting.

Photography again got Menken in trouble, this time with Swinburne. (Victoria and Albert Museum)

By the summer of 1868, she had lost too much weight and energy and collapsed during a rehearsal. On August 10, 1868, she died of an abdominal abscess. Gerson contended that Dumas and three of Adah's servants were the only mourners at her funeral. Her estate was bankrupt, and she was initially buried in a Parisian cemetery for paupers. Lesser believed that Adah's son had died some months before, but Gerson wrote that he was alive at his mother's death. The latter account indicates that the child was adopted and renamed after Adah's burial. Obviously the end of her life was as shrouded in mystery as the beginning.

Adah seems to have cared less than her sister actresses for quality legitimate theater or the development of her own talents as a serious tragic or comic actress. It is hard to believe, for all her literary pretentions, that she loved the "theater" or "drama." She was much more the star, the stage phenomenon, interested in developing physical prowess or the shocking, cute routine that packed the houses. The theater was as much a vehicle by which Adah fed her hungry ego as it was a means by which Mary Ann Duff fed her children. One gets the impression that if Adah could have gotten the attention and fame she demanded in any other way besides the theater, she might just as easily have taken that other way. As it was, some theatrical people believed that, in her role of Mazeppa particularly, she brought a new freedom to the actress. In the view of many of her fellow professionals, however, she had in her private life simply proven the worst myths that critics of the theater had insisted on promulgating about all actresses; thus she made the education of an antagonistic public even more difficult. Had this unintended damage to the professionalism of the stage been done by a great actress like Duff or Keene, then it surely would have been easier for her critics in the profession to swallow, but the stereotype was reinforced by one who was primarily interested in tricks and spectacle.

In the final analysis The Menken was probably more sinned against than sinner, having merely determined to be what society accused her of being anyway. Finding that society often showered rewards when it did not bestow approval, she preferred the rewards. It would be difficult for even her harshest critics to ignore the immense vitality, courage, and intelligence of Adah Menken. In many ways, both personally and professionally, she was in the avant garde, as few others were. With the natural, graceful use of her body, she defied the ingrained artificial priggishness in the theater. She also broadened the classic play and melodrama of the legitimate theater by incorporating other arts as diverse as painting, sculpture, and circus performance into her productions.

She cared very much about other art and artists of her time. She never stopped thinking of herself as a serious poet, and she recognized and sought out literary genius wherever she was. That Dumas, Dickens, Swinburne, Rossetti, and others valued her company indicates something of her intelligence and fire.

Few prominent actors had to face such a degree of personal excoriation at the hands of the public, such painful turns of fate in private life, and such essential loneliness. Yet she weathered it all to the very end with an indomitable spirit.

# _CHAPTER 9_

# LOTTA CRABTREE

A child of the American West, Charlotte ("Lotta") Crabtree (1847-1924) was the most thoroughly American of the successful actresses of the nineteenth century. Born in 1847 in New York City and reared from the age of five in California towns, she learned her trade in mining camps, on San Francisco stages, and from American minstrels. Any story of Lotta, including Constance Rourke's fine *Troupers of the Gold Coast,* has to be devoted largely to Lotta's mother, Mary Ann Crabtree, who planned Lotta's life, trained her, put her on the stage, and closely managed her personal life and finances until after Lotta's retirement at forty-five. Lotta's father was a ne'er-do-well bartender who left the family in New York without means so that he could hunt for gold in California in 1852. When he wrote his family to join him in the West, his wife, Mary Ann, was not surprised that he neglected to tell her where to find him or to enclose any money for their passage. Nevertheless, Mary Ann and five-year-old Lotta managed to reach San Francisco and eventually found Crabtree in a California mining camp. Those first few days in San Francisco, before Mary Ann found Crabtree, profoundly changed the course of the life of the child with her, for it was at this time that Mary Ann was inspired to shape her daughter's life in a particular way. She was struck by the popularity of child stars, especially the little Bateman girls and Sue Robinson, who played mining camps as

Lotta Crabtree, who began performing as a child, retained her childlike quality for many years. (Harvard Theatre Collection)

161

well as San Francisco theaters. Constance Rourke speculated on what must have gone through Mary Ann's mind as she viewed the lively theatrical scene in light of what she felt were her daughter's undeveloped talents:

> To Mary Ann Crabtree, watching and judging, this spectacle might have been disheartening: but with the rise of Mrs. Sinclair one conclusion must have been borne in upon her. The prizes were going to women. In this new world composed preponderantly of men, women were rising to a singular eminence. For months all the drift of interest on stage had been toward women, Caroline Chapman, Lola Montez, Matilda Heron, Laura Keene, Catherine Sinclair, besides the singers Biscaccianti, Kate Hayes, and now Anna Bishop. . . . If the stage in California was still a gusty affair, full of dangerous, sudden changes, it offered an unparalleled opportunity for feminine initiative.[1]

The observation of the San Francisco theater scene in these first three days determined their lives, for as soon as the family was settled, Mary Ann saw that Lotta had lessons in singing and dancing. Prospects looked good for a future in entertainment even in their temporary home in the Grass Valley mining camp, which supported a theater troupe, a playhouse, a company of child performers, and a number of saloons with stages where entertainers, including Lola Montez, performed. Lola, a colorful woman who had made a fortune and a worldwide reputation by dancing, was also an inspiration of sorts to Mary Ann. She was able to shield her daughter from what she regarded as Montez's moral taint and at the same time see that Lotta learned something of the stage from the notorious siren.

However, it was Mart Taylor, a tavern owner in Grass Valley, rather than Lola Montez, who was most responsible for educating Lotta for the stage. By the time the child was seven, not only was she a well-known stage performer in Grass Valley, but Taylor and her mother often took her to other mining camps to entertain. Often during Crabtree's many unaccountable absences, Mary Ann, Taylor, Lotta, and her little brother rode on horseback to play other mining camps characterized by violence and primitive living conditions. The way was so perilous that at one time a man riding ahead of Lotta slipped and fell with his horse to his death. Often, the only sleep that Lotta got was in the saddle onto which she was carefully tied. At one stop, when a brawl broke out in their "hotel," the family was forced to sleep on the floor of their room in order to dodge the bullets whizzing through the canvas walls. In such camps as this, Lotta, who was about seven, played in canvas-covered halls, furnished only with benches, before an audience in which a wrong move on the part of a performer could send the miners, gamblers, and other ruffians into full-scale riot. And quite often the only pay Lotta received was money thrown onto the stage by the spectators, who loved to see the child scramble to pick it up. Nevertheless, as time passed, such appearances often proved very profitable. Sometimes among the trinkets showered on the popular child were solid-gold watches.

As usual, Crabtree, her father, could be expected to act selfishly: when the seven-year-old Lotta appeared to be doing well, he secretly sold her to a group of traveling actors who left town with her. Mary Ann, in despair and heavy with child, had to send the sheriff to locate and return her daughter. Referring to Lotta's father and brothers, David K. Dempsey wrote in a study of Lotta that, for her, "men would be obstacles to, rather than the means of survival."[2]

When Lotta was nine, Mary Ann thought that she was ready to be moved to the city, San Francisco. Even the best of California theaters in 1854 were violent places. Lotta started out performing in the worst of them—the roughest kind of waterfront establishments, notorious for their nightly shootings, knifings, and brawls; and in the basements of melodeons where few women, and then only the lowest prostitutes, were ever seen. Despite this, or maybe because of it, Mary Ann was the strictest of chaperones. Lotta was never out of her sight. Furthermore, the stage mother unfailingly informed all managers, even of the worst establishments, that if one vulgar word reached Lotta's ears, they were to consider the contract broken. Her protection of her child was as fierce for all the rest of Lotta's life.

At twelve years of age, Lotta moved up to a one-night stand as the youngest member of Tom Macguire's San Francisco company. But Macguire already had other child actors and did not hire her for additional performances. Mary Ann was not satisfied with the rate of her daughter's advancement in the city, so she arranged for Lotta to go on tour with a minstrel troupe. The influence on Lotta of the minstrel shows, which were playing all over California at this time, was a lasting one. Most of her performances for the rest of her career included banjo playing, breakdown dances, and even comic routines played in blackface. Her success in minstrelry was unusual in that it was then, and continued to be, largely an all-male entertainment.

Mary Ann had been a quick student of all she had seen of the craft she encouraged Lotta to master, and she was able, by the time Lotta

Lotta Crabtree in a favorite role as a mischievous young boy. (George C.D. Odell, *Annals of the New York Stage*. Columbia University Press. Reprinted with permission.)

was in her teens, to be the girl's most perceptive coach. Rourke described one instance during the mining camp tour of 1859 of Mary Ann's teaching Lotta to "milk" an otherwise insignificant scene:

> Her coach was her mother, who knew nothing about the theater except what she had learned from quick and curious observation during her two brief sojourns in San Francisco, or from traveling players whom she had chanced to see in Grass Valley, or during the long hard jaunt of the summer before. But she understood sharply studied effects. Somehow she knew what would draw laughter; and she knew how to arouse the spirit of laughter in her little girl. In one play Lotta had only to place a bottle on a table. Mrs. Crabtree taught her to peer from the wings, to withdraw, set one foot forward, to walk across the stage bearing the bottle with exaggerated dignity, and then to laugh—with a look at the audience—as she set it down. It was the inconsequent quick laugh—so unexpectedly hearty for her size—and the companionable glance that drew a response.

After the first performance an older actress demanded the part; but Mrs. Crabtree had stipulated that Lotta was to keep it, and she not only could make a bargain, she could enforce one. Lotta continued to walk on with the bottle, added a jig step as she set it down, and turned a handspring as she reached the wings again.[3]

When Mrs. Crabtree returned to the city, she and her company were ignored by the kingmaker of California entertainers, Tom Macguire. Macguire even made the mistake of disparaging Lotta's act when Crabtree put in one of his rare appearances in the family circle. At this time, he made what was perhaps his only contribution to the development of his daughter's career: he shot Macguire in the arm in reprisal for the unflattering remark. The event did nothing to hasten Macguire's acceptance of Lotta, but the publicity won another engagement for her in a low dancehall theater of the city. However, this too ended after a few weeks, and Lotta and Mary Ann went out on tour once again. Mary Ann still had not won the battle with the prestige theaters of San Francisco, but one positive effect of the continual touring, aside from the invaluable stage experience it afforded, was Lotta's growing popularity among people of the towns and mining camps throughout California, many of whom came to make up San Francisco audiences.

When Lotta returned to the city for the second time in 1859, Macguire could no longer ignore her. This time she was given a place in his legitimate house and star billing as well. One other certain measure of her success in San Francisco was the invitation to play benefits for the San Francisco fire brigades. It was during these years, from 1859 to 1864, that Lotta developed the programs from which she rarely deviated. She played the parts of young boys, making waifs and orphans her specialties. She also perfected the minstrel-show routine, the farce, the burlesques of serious plays, and the musicals that came to be expected of her. Comedies were written especially for Lotta. She remained at the top of her profession on the West Coast until 1864, when she was seventeen; at that time she left to conquer New York. She had become a star of such magnitude that her farewell benefit brought her $1,500.

New Yorkers, not quite ready for Lotta, did not share the enthusiasm of Californians. Her first appearance was a failure. So once more Mary Ann took Lotta to the provinces. Only after a highly successful tour of the Midwest and of small eastern cities and an appearance in Chicago could she return as a star to New York. At Wallacks she played to packed houses, often appearing in thirteen plays in as many nights. On some evenings she took as many as six different roles. The *Times* reported that she "conveniently forgets . . . her sex to imitate a very far gone state of tipsiness. . . . Her natural smartness needs but to be cultivated to make her the most sparkling actress of our age."[4]

By the late 1860s and early 1870s, success was total and complete, and she was all the rage wherever she went—St. Louis, Chicago, Albany, Boston—everywhere on the theatrical circuit. At nineteen she was wealthy, supporting her family in high style and giving the money from her benefits to charity. At Wallacks Theater her share of the receipts—$10,000 for twenty-eight days—was typical.

Several aspects of her life were very peculiar. The strangest, especially in view of the daring, unconventional characters she assumed on stage, were her dependence on her mother and her failure to develop any romantic relationships. Lotta was now making all the artistic decisions, but Mary Ann handled all the money singlehandedly from the beginning to the end of Lotta's career and until she died, after Lotta had retired. She was a strong woman, and experience had taught her to be demanding. Her custom was to insist on being paid in advance, usually in cash. She trusted no one and kept large sums of money and bonds in a strong box in her room. Even as a very old lady, Mary Ann comforted herself by sitting alone outside Lotta's bedroom, jingling coins in her lap. Although it was Lotta who made the money, who saw that large amounts of it were given to charity—often to clothe an army of urchins in any city where she played—and Lotta in whose name huge investments were made, it was Mary Ann who actually managed the money and who invested it all. Lotta rarely even saw any money, let alone spent any. Up until Lotta was a fifty-year-old woman, Mary Ann never advanced her more than a nickel at a time. In her memoir, *Lotta's Last Season,* Helen Marie Bates, a woman with Lotta's company, told of an incident that illustrates Mary Ann's practice of controlling Lotta's money. Lotta, who was in her forties at the time, discovered one afternoon after rehearsal that she had no money to get home, so she asked the stage manager, a Mr. Dunn, if she could borrow ten cents for a trolley ride. Mr. Dunn readily provided her with a dollar bill, but Lotta lost the dollar before she got home. The next day Mary Ann stormed up to Mr. Dunn to repay the dollar: "'Mr. Dunn, Miss Lotta told me that you gave her a dollar the other day, a dollar which she promptly lost. Never again give her more than ten cents *at one time*. She has no knowledge of money, never has need of it.'"[5]

On another occasion, Lotta, in her forties, was left in the care of Miss Bates in Chicago when Mary Ann had to be away from her on business. The two women decided to amuse themselves by shopping and, as Bates remembered it, Lotta went wild in Chicago's Marshall Field's, ordering and charging everything that her heart desired, like a child on a buying binge. When Mary Ann returned, she scolded Bates for allowing the shopping trip to occur and informed her that she had returned to Marshall Field's every article that Lotta had bought. Only when Mary Ann realized that her own death was imminent did she set about systematically to educate Lotta in money matters. Lotta at this time was almost fifty and had retired from the stage.

That Lotta learned to be independent and learned well, is something of a miracle, for Mary Ann had closely overseen all aspects of Lotta's life, not just her financial affairs. On those rare occasions when she had to leave Lotta alone, even when Lotta was in middle age, Mary Ann had made sure that another woman like Miss Bates was left in charge of her, even leaving orders that a female member of the staff was always to accompany Lotta every time she left her rooms. Bates recalled Mary Ann's words when Lotta was left in someone else's charge: "Lotta is a veritable child who never has done things like older women. She has been sheltered, cared for and has no idea of the value of money nor what it will buy. I have kept her that way and never consult her in regard to business outside the theater."[6]

Lotta's love life, or lack of one, was also in large measure attributable to the effectiveness of her mother's efforts in running off all suitors. Bates insisted that "Mrs. Crabtree was a man-hater. Lotta was guarded like an odalisque in a harem."[7] Hence the young Lotta came to be called "Lotta, the Unapproachable." There were rumors once in a while that she was in love, but no relationship ever got very far. Supposedly she was enamored of Dexter Smith, editor of a small music magazine, but her mother quickly put an end to the courtship. When a rich Philadelphian named J. Bolton Hulme paid court to Lotta, Mary Ann was able to send him packing when she discovered that he drank and had gambled with some of Lotta's money. There were others: a Harvard student whose father broke off the friendship when he became afraid that his son would marry an actress, and an entrepreneur named Henry E. Abbey who married someone else after Lotta had backed his career as a stage manager.

Part of the reason why she had no serious love affair and never married was obviously Mary Ann, and part of the reason was doubtless her own single-minded devotion to her career with the necessary traveling, which allowed little or no time for a romance to develop. Both Rourke and Bates are inclined to attribute her single life to a kind of fickleness as well. Lotta was quoted by Bates as saying, "I have a fickle nature. I care for no one or anything very long, and once they are gone, I never miss them or feel sadness at their passing. I enjoy change."[8] She implied that she could not sustain interest in any one man. Another of Lotta's biographers, David Dempsey, believed that she lacked some sense of nineteenth-century romance, at least as it was reflected in the plays she knew: "To her, stage love, as it came across the footlights of the day, *was* ridiculous. In all her later triumphs she mocked it, sometimes with a wink, more often with a kick, and always with an inimitable sense of being Lotta, of standing outside the play and laughing at it."[9]

Whatever the truth of those allegations, it is impossible to escape another reason for Lotta's failure to marry: the few males with which she was allowed to have contact, her father and brothers, were scarcely conducive to a healthy regard for the opposite sex. Crabtree was irresponsible, an emotional and economic drain on Mary Ann. In California he would get drunk for long periods of time, disappear without a word for months, and always gamble away whatever money he could get from his wife. In New York, he was equally undependable and destructive. The actor Walter Leman records one instance when Mary Ann and Lotta, at the height of the actress's success, waited hours alone backstage like forlorn waifs for Crabtree to escort them home. When it became clear that he was never going to appear, they got home by themselves and then, because they were locked out of the house, had to wait on the doorstep until dawn for Crabtree to return home from his carousing and let them in. Relations with Crabtree grew more and more intolerable after they left California. Mary Ann had him arrested for breaking into her strongbox and stealing Lotta's money, and by the late sixties his debauchery and deliberate interference were threatening Lotta's reputation. In 1872, he got what he wanted. Mary Ann set him up with a pub in Liverpool and gave him a healthy allowance with Lotta's money.

Lotta's two brothers followed in their father's footsteps. Lotta financed their fly-by-night schemes, bailed them out of shady business deals, covered their gambling debts, and supported their mistresses from the time she was in her early twenties until long after Mary Ann's death. When, in old age, she was asked how much money she had lavished on her father and brothers, she said that a conservative estimate would be a million dollars.

In any case, Lotta's most intimate view of marriage was not exactly a happy one. The subject of her sex life, or lack of it, continued to be an issue even after she had died at the age of seventy-seven. When a young woman claiming to be Lotta's daughter stepped forward to collect the actress's vast estate, medical evidence was introduced to prove that Lotta had lived and died a virgin.

Lotta's mother always shielded her from what she considered to be immoral behavior. She had been careful to keep Lotta clear of stage associates in California. Not only was she never allowed to have friends among show people, but she was rarely even seen in informal backstage conversation. Mary Ann saw that Lotta spent no more time in the theater than was absolutely necessary. Nor did Bates notice that any change had occurred when she worked with Lotta some thirty years later. All members of Lotta's company were invariably screened carefully by Mary Ann, and the women's quarters were separated from the men's whenever the show was touring. Furthermore, men and women were expected to be fully dressed whenever they left their quarters.

If Lotta had not been a lady, it would have been over Mary Ann's dead body; but the older woman seems to have allowed her daughter a number of eccentricities unbefitting a Victorian lady. Lotta, for example, was famous for smoking cigars in public and onstage. She also insisted on wearing her dresses much shorter than was considered proper in order to show off her ankles. Apparently she got rid of much psychological pressure with her strenuous highjinks onstage. There she was outrageously flirtatious, kicked her heels high, danced wildly, cursed, and played the banjo to the breaking point. The great irony was that her stage rowdiness had all the daring that her private life completely lacked. Rourke described the rare style that Mary Ann helped her to develop.

> The hoyden in a dozen aspects became Lotta's substantial part. She rolled off sofas and showed far more than an ankle; pulling up her stocking she ran out onto the stage in *Nan the Good for Nothing*. The movement, in an age when even allusions to stockings were considered depraved, became indescribably comic. She lifted herself to tables and swung her feet—another dashing innovation. Her short skirts were daring, as was her smoking. [10]

When Lotta was forty-five she was still playing boys and saucy little girls. During a performance that year when she threw herself backwards into the arms of an actor, the movement was so energetic that he collapsed, allowing her to fall to the stage and break a vertebra. Following the accident, she decided to retire. From that time on she devoted herself completely to the ailing Mary Ann as she had once devoted herself to the stage. Mary Ann died when Lotta was sixty years old, leaving $70,000 in cash hidden around the house.

In her retirement years Lotta gave vent to numerous interests and eccentricities. For a few years she was amused by raising and racing horses. She invested in a hotel and ran it herself, learned to drive a car, went to meetings for her favorite charities, made a project of producing hats for city horses, and most of all, spent hour after hour working on her will, which, despite all her care, was contested in one of the most bizarre series of trials imaginable. In the last year of her life she was the second largest taxpayer in Boston, and she left an estate of $4 million.

No other successful actress in the century was so thoroughly American, so little directly influenced by the English and European stages. Kemble, Keene and Duff were first educated to the British theater. Menken felt herself to be another Byron, inspired by the European bohemianism of Montez. Mowatt had had the English education of a child of wealth. Cushman only flowered in England and found the

Lotta's scandalous cigar smoking belied her innocence. (Harvard Theatre Collection)

English style suitable for her. But Lotta was the child of the Far West. Although the English music hall must have indirectly influenced her, the theater that reached her was filtered through the American frontier, and almost every one of her acts had the indelible stamp of the thoroughly American minstrel show.

One thinks of her as a child sleeping tied to the saddle of her horse; of her seeing the horse and rider ahead of her on the trail slip and fall to their deaths; of her lying on the floor of a mining camp hotel as bullets whizzed through the canvas walls; of her following the bawdiest of mining camp acts; of her playing in low dance halls too sordid for most women and too dangerous for most men; of her friendship with two of the most notorious women of the century; of her complete absorption in a profession considered to be beyond the pale of respectability; of the reprobate lives of the male members of the family. Considered in this environment, her essential innocence and her rigidly sheltered life are extraordinary. Although Lotta's acting supported the family, she was as thoroughly protected from the world outside her very limited sphere as any American Nora in a Victorian household. A better analogy might be Hawthorne's Hilda in *The Marble Faun;* Lotta walked through some of the wildest and most sordid aspects of nineteenth-century life without being touched by them. Her life is a paradox of purity and tawdriness.

There is also a paradox in the fact that this innocent woman's innovation and rebellion formed a much more fundamental reach for equality as an artist than did the almost-nude appearance of Menken, an actress with a reputation for rebellion. Constance Rourke wrote:

> Broad comedy for women was still rebellious. In a period when a delicate distance was considered an ultimate feminine quality, it was rebellion indeed to forget the prerogative of a languishing charm; it was nothing short of revolt to diminish the aura by which women—it was hoped— might always be surrounded, and actually to laugh at an audience, thus shattering distance altogether. Few actresses even in the liberal California days had attempted it, even though a tradition for comedy had prevailed there.[11]

While Menken exploited and was exploited by nineteenth-century sexism, Lotta seemed to have been outside it—even beyond it.

# CHAPTER 10

# CONCLUSION

The study of a small group of people who were truly isolated from the mainstream of their society has for us some of the prurient appeal of a sideshow. We in the twentieth century stand like the nineteenth-century fat man in the pit, gawking at a woman in the costume of a man who thunders across the stage with a foil and addresses words of love to another actress. We are fascinated by the anomaly, Dr. Johnson's metaphoric dog walking on its hind legs. To study her is to relish the excitement of the unexpected that we so often find in the underside of American history. The significant curiosity in such a study, however, is not the woman dressed as a man; it is the age itself—an age that castigated its members for exercising the full range of their human faculties. Disapproval of the theater, arising partly from the memory of abuses of the Restoration stage, was particularly severe in a country where Calvinistic mistrust of all art was slow to die, even a century after the established Puritan church had breathed its last breath. But the legacy continued to affect the American view of art; the imagination and emotions were shameful, deceptive, and dangerous faculties that must be denied or, if they should rear their ugly heads, immediately repressed. The perils of the imagination arose from its power to conjure up images not found in nature. With its use, human beings could play God and create a deceptive world where the realities of divine

Pauline Markham. (George C.D. Odell, *Annals of the New York Stage.* Columbia University Press. Reprinted with permission.)

retribution for human error might be denied, where sin, as the Victorian defined it, could be made attractive and exercised with impunity. In the pride-engendered, false world of the imagination, the thief could be honorable, the harlot justified. The weak human character, deceived by such a world, might leave behind the restrictions of Victorian reality, the mores of the Victorians' own culture, which they interpreted as divine and eternal dictates. Without these restrictions, the human being, exposed to a creation of the imagination, was subject to all the darker impulses—self-indulgence, heresy, nonconformity, bohemianism, passion, sensuality—all of which had previously lain throbbing beneath the surface of the character liable at any moment to burst free.

Of all the arts, the theater posed the most serious peril because it was living, immediate, graphic. Ministers who had come to tolerate the reading of fiction and poetry, even the reading of plays, continued to disapprove of the theater, for it instantly summoned to life a counterfeit world, encouraging sensations of which proper Victorians would ordinarily feel ashamed. That many people could not distinguish the world outside the theater from that created onstage was a point made repeatedly by the clergy. The dangers of being utterly deceived by a fabrication, often confusing false values with true ones, would often be illustrated by clergymen with the story of a woman in the audience who fainted at a crucial point in the action of a play or the bumpkin who jumped onstage from the audience to save the heroine.

Victorian fear of the creative imagination, particularly as it was so graphically displayed onstage, illustrates the culture's repudiation of the full range of human faculties. The Victorian attitude toward the emotions and imagination is no less apparent in its attitude toward women. Society openly gave its approval to the pure mother-wife who, though she may have known defilement of the flesh in the cause of procreation, had never been tainted by sexual desire, never awakened to sensualty. And to be less than snow-white was to be scarlet. Underlying the Victorian necessity for restrictions upon woman's senses, imagination, passion, even thought was the conviction that a woman was both weak and dangerous, that these elements were, in truth, throbbing with great intensity beneath that snow-white female breast, ready at the least provocation, at the least relaxation of rigid social restrictions, to tear loose and precipitate a repetition of the Eve-produced lapse, bringing about the downfall of the Victorian world or, at the very least, a Victorian Adam.

Thus, at the root of the American distrust of art, particularly as its dangers were magnified in the theater, was the same apprehension that led Victorians to wrap up their women, body and soul: fear of the creative principle that, in the hands of artist or woman, could summon up devilishness to threaten nineteenth-century order. In this sense, woman and art were one. Whether or not the connection was openly acknowledged, this deadly kinship felt between art and female nature left Victorians uneasy in the presence of both.

So, as both woman and artist, the actress was under a double curse in her society. Joining with a pernicious art her darker, uncontrolled female faculties of imagination and emotion, unchecked by reason as they were in the male, she lured husbands away from the hearths of good women and lured women away from the path to salvation.

Perhaps it was in part the outcast status shared by woman and the theater—certainly it was that common, despised creative principle—that brought together the theater and women seeking careers. The potential, however subdued, for the exercise of the creative imagination and the emotions, which society contemned in womankind, were precisely those qualities on which theatrical art depended. So what was feared outside the theater as woman's secret nature was fostered within the theater. Moreover, the talent for creating an intense emotional display was particularly appreciated by Americans: the intense, noncerebral style of Mrs. Duff, the instant tears of the emotional school, the uninhibited highjinks of Lotta, all appeared to be more valued on the nineteenth-century American stage than the highly restrained, carefully balanced, analytical performance in which rationality was more in evidence than feeling.

The differences between the theater and the mainstream of society made the theater a true subculture. Religious Americans could not by law forbid the setting up of theaters as their ancestors had done in the eighteenth century, but they did what they could to keep theatrical people at a distance and to ensure the actor's station as outcast. Eventually the theater became like an island, separated from the rest of the world by a different evolution, isolated, and with values and lives distinct from those of other people. Theatrical people did not even eat, sleep, and work when all the rest of the country ate, slept, and worked. Their hours were irregular. They worked at night and slept in the morning. They frequently lived on the road, remaining for only a few nights in a hotel before moving on. The tools of their trade were so much witchery: costumes from different eras, including padding, and makeup which, worn on the street, identified the whore. At a time when the decent person shunned the use of the word *leg* and when it was not laughable to cover the legs of pianos to avoid untoward suggestion, actors and actresses of good repute appeared onstage in tights. When to be seen riding in a carriage with a member of the opposite sex meant either betrothal or scandal and a kiss was tantamount to a lifelong commitment in some quarters, actors and actresses readily embraced one another onstage as their roles demanded. When young women were warned not to work in factories also employing men, actresses and actors dressed, rehearsed, and traveled with one another. At a time when a glimpse on the street of a woman of questionable reputation was enough to make the ordinary woman faint with shame, the actress appeared nightly in an establishment hospitable to large numbers of prostitutes.

As a consequence of its being so drastically divorced from the rest of society in mores as well as values, the theater became a small counterculture in many ways; paradoxically, at the same time that its very purpose was often to produce onstage a miniature of the Victorian world, theatrical society offstage was a mirror inversion of Victorian society. In no other way was this inversion so pronounced as in the theater's treatment of women. Women in the theater were not subject to the limitations placed upon them by Victorians, and the theater placed on women expectations that Victorians scorned. In the theater women took on the roles usually reserved for men. They assumed the support of their families, often accumulating considerable wealth; they became formidable voices within the planning sessions of companies and frequently assumed entire control of large businesses. They borrowed money, invested, rented establishments, constructed buildings, arranged tours, hired men and women, paid salaries, and fired employees—this when other women were kept in complete ignorance of money matters. Obviously women succeeded in performing tasks and assuming responsibilities in the theatrical subculture that society at large believed that women should not do—indeed, could not do.

The actress, who was so often on stage against her choice, found herself free of the moral expectations of the larger community simply because it had given up on her. As soon as she had stepped through the forbidden portals into the theater, she had little left of her good name, little of her good reputation to lose. For example, she no longer worried about polite society's admonitions against women working side by side with men or coming into physical contact with men. The chaste Lotta had nothing to lose by smoking her cigars in public and flashing her ankle, and Charlotte Cushman hesitated not at all to dress in male trousers and boots—attire that would have shamed other women.

The actress also found that she was no longer bound by sexual stereotypes, whether she liked the situation or not. The theater ignored the idea that women were fragile, frail, and helpless, without the strength to honestly earn their own way. Theatrical life, especially when it involved traveling, demanded considerable discipline and physical stamina from its men and its women equally. Memoirs of managers Ludlow and Smith and of actors Wallack and Jefferson betray no hint that companies took into account the delicacy of their female members. Indeed, when violence had emptied an audience of women spectators, actresses usually stood their ground onstage as long as the men did, often being wounded with flying furniture and, on occasion, ammunition.

The theater's un-Victorian view of women contributed to the ironic direction taken by the actresses' personal lives. At the same time that an actress gained the freedom and independence with which her Victorian counterparts were unfamiliar, she usually lost the chance for a harmonious, society-approved marriage. Mary Ann Crabtree and Charlotte Cushman realized what many actresses found out too late, that marriage, especially to someone outside the profession, would not be compatible with a career. The freedom of the theater and that inversion of Victorian values to which actresses became accustomed were rarely understood by nonprofessionals. Even after relinquishing careers for marriages, Fanny Kemble and Anna Cora Mowatt were obviously unable to adjust to the accepting, subservient positions required of ordinary women. The closest most actresses came to ordinary domestic happiness was in the roles they played repeatedly onstage.

Another irony in the life of the actress was found in her relationship to the "real" world of politics and business. Ministers condemned the theater as a place of make-believe, and they saw to it that the stage remained removed from acceptable society. Yet these women who made their living in a world of pretense were, with the exceptions of domesticity and religion, more in touch with reality than those ordinary women of the century who lived as dolls in dollhouses.

Mrs. Drew, Laura Keene, and all the other "petticoat governors" and actresses of the century are phenomena in the context of their times. In an age when most women rarely emerged from the home, when they accepted universally and unquestioningly their subservience to men, when a physician supposedly speaking in their defense would insist that women should not even teach except as assistants to men— in such an age there existed a despised subculture where women could work, aspire, compete equally with men and other women for money and influence. Here were women in positions of considerable power: unlike other women in the century, the actress was not on a pedestal, nor, to mix a metaphor, was she behind the throne. At this time, in this special place, she was herself on the throne.

# _NOTES_

## Chapter 1.  Enter the Harlot

A picture of the nature and extent of nineteenth-century antagonism toward the theater can be found in general cultural and theatrical histories as well as in tracts, editorials, books, and articles written by the people here listed, each of whom is noted in the bibliography that follows the chapter notes: David Agnew, Henry Ward Beecher, James Buckley, William Clapp, William Davidge, William Dunlap, Timothy Dwight, William Everts, George Gouley, Phineas Gurley, Robert Hatfield, Stephen Hill, Philip Hone, Joseph Jefferson, Jeremiah Jeter, Herrick Johnson, Taylor Lewis, Olive Logan, Noah Ludlow, J. H. McVicker, Clara Morris, Anna Cora Mowatt, A. M. Palmer, Sol Smith, Thomas DeWitt Talmadge, Francis Trollope, Robert Turnbull, John T. Ware, Samuel Winchester, and William Wood.

1. Clara Morris, *Life on the Stage; My Personal Experiences and Recollections* (New York, 1901), p. 7.

2. Albert M. Palmer, "American Theaters," in *One Hundred Years of American Commerce,* vol. 1, ed. Chauncey M. Depew (New York, 1895), p. 157.

3. William Dunlap, *History of the American Theater,* (1832; reprint: New York, 1963), pp. 23-27.

4. Ibid., pp. 120-23. See also R. S., "To the Printer," *New York Journal,* 28 January 1768, no. 1308, p. 2.

5. Dunlap, *History of the American Theater,* pp. 120-23.

6. Ibid., pp. ˙242-52.

7. Sidney E. Ahlstrom, *The Religious History of the American People* (New Haven, 1972), p. 470.

8. Alexis de Tocqueville, *Democracy in America,* vol. 1 (1853; reprint: New York, 1951), pp. 305, 306.

9. Thomas Colley Grattan, *Civilized America,* vol. 2 (1859; reprint: New York, 1969), p. 340.

10. Winthrop S. Hudson, *American Protestantism* (Chicago, 1961), p. 96.

11. Ibid., p. 96.

12. Frances Trollope, *Domestic Manners of the Americans* (1828; reprint: New York, 1949), p. 107.

13. Ibid., p. 77.

14. Hudson, *American Protestantism,* p. 110.

15. G. Lewis, *Impressions of America and the American Churches* (1848; reprint: New York, 1968), p. 406.

16. Hudson, *American Protestantism,* pp. 109, 110.

17. James Monroe Buckley, *Christians and the Theatre* (New York, 1875), pp. 16-18; Gaillard Hunt, *Life in America* (New York, 1914), p. 88; David Grimsted, *Melodrama Unveiled* (Chicago, 1968), p. 25.

18. Timothy Dwight, *An Essay on the Stage* (Middletown, Conn., 1824), p. 101.

19. Henry Ward Beecher, *Lectures to Young Men* (New York, 1856), p. 235.

20. Robert M. Hatfield, *The Theatre* (Chicago, 1866), pp. 27, 28.

21. DeWitt Talmadge, *Sports That Kill* (New York, 1875), p. 17.

22. Herrick Johnson, *A Plain Talk about the Theater* (Chicago, 1882), p. 19.

23. Talmadge, *Sports*, p. 18.

24. William B. Wood, *Personal Recollections of the Stage* (Philadelphia, 1855), p. 208.

25. Noah Ludlow, *Dramatic Life as I Found It* (St. Louis, 1880), p. 347.

26. Sol Smith, *Theatrical Management in the South and West* (New York, 1868), p. 60.

27. Maud Skinner, *One Man in His Time: the Adventures of H. Watkins, Strolling Player, 1845-1863* (Philadelphia, 1938), p. 38.

28. Ibid., p. 47.

29. Joseph Jefferson, *The Autobiography of Joseph Jefferson* (New York, 1889), pp. 252, 253.

30. William Winter, *The Wallet of Time* (New York, 1913) p. 57.

31. John Hodgkinson, *A Narrative of His Connection with the Old America Company* (New York, 1797), p. 22.

32. Philip Hone, *The Diary of Philip Hone, 1828–1851,* ed. Allan Nevins (New York, 1936), p. 573.

33. Ibid., p. 348.

34. Trollope, *Domestic Manners,* p. 564; J. S. Buckingham, *The Eastern and Western States of America,* vol. 2 (London, 1842), p. 395.

35. Palmer, "American Theaters," p. 165.

36. Daniel Frohman, *Daniel Frohman Presents* (New York, 1935), p. 44.

37. Hatfield, *The Theatre,* p. 24.

38. Anna Cora Mowatt, *Autobiography of an Actress* (Boston, 1854), p. 214.

39. Ibid., p. 445.

40. Clara Morris, *Stage Confidences* (Boston, 1902), pp. 13, 14.

41. Ibid., p. 33.

42. Ibid., p. 31.

43. Smith, *Theatrical Management,* p. 175.

44. Claire McGlinchee, *The First Decade of the Boston Museum* (Boston, 1940), pp. 24, 25.

45. Richard Moody, ed., *Dramas from the American Theater, 1762–1909* (New York, 1966), pp. 349–59.

46. Ahlstrom, *Religious History,* p. 731; Ann Douglass, *The Feminization of American Culture* (New York, 1977), pp. 17–49.

47. Daniel Howe, "Victorian Culture in America," in *Victorian America* ed. Daniel Howe (Philadelphia, 1976), pp. 25, 26.

48. Ibid., pp. 3–28; Martha L. Rayne, *What Can a Woman Do?* (n.d.; reprint: New York, 1974), pp. 295–310. Other books on the family-centered values of the time include Edward Westermarck, *The Origin and Development of the Moral Ideas* (New York, 1906); Alexander M. Gow, *Good Morals and Gentle Manners for Schools and Families* (New York, 1873); Katherine Kish Sklar, *Catherine Beecher: A Study in American Domesticity* (New Haven, 1973).

49. Mowatt, *Autobiography,* p. 445; Dunlap, *History of the American Theater,* pp. 407–412; Ludlow, *Dramatic Life,* pp. 478–79; Olive Logan, *Before the Footlights and behind the Scene* (Philadelphia, 1870), pp. 33-35.

50. Claudia D. Johnson, "That Guilty Third Tier," in *Victorian America* ed. Daniel Howe (Philadelphia, 1976), p. 113.

51. Dunlap, *History of the American Theater,* pp. 407–412.

52. J. J. Jennings, *Theatrical and Circus Life* (St. Louis, 1882), pp. 60–65.

53. John M. Murtagh and Sara Harris, *Cast the First Stone* (New York, 1957), p. 205.

54. Logan, *Before the Footlights,* p. 540; Robert Turnbull, *The Theatre* (Hartford, 1837), p. 84.

55. "A Letter to Respectable Ladies Who Frequent the Theater." *The Christian Spectator* 1, August 1827, p. 411.

56. "The Theatre," *New York Morning Herald,* 1 November 1842, p. 2.

57. Ludlow, *Dramatic Life,* p. 479.

58. "Ladies of New York Look Well to This Thing," *New York Morning Herald,* 19 September 1838, p. 2.

59. Talmadge, *Sports,* p. 44.

60. Ibid., p. 22

61. Logan, *Before the Footlights,* p. 537.

62. "A Letter to Respectable Ladies," pp. 412, 413.

63. Stephen P. Hill, *Theatrical Amusements* (Philadelphia, 1830), p. 18.

64. Ibid., p. 18.

65. Turnbull, pp. 85–89.

66. William W. Sanger, *A History of Prostitution: Its Extent, Causes and Effects throughout the World* (New York, 1858), p. 557.

67. Ibid., p. 597.

68. Murtagh and Harris, *Cast the First Stone,* p. 205.

69. Turnbull, *The Theatre,* p. 80.

70. William Everts, *The Theatre,* (Chicago, 1866), p. 42.

71. J. C. Furnas, *The Americans: A Social History of the United States* (New York, 1969), p. 504.

72. Ibid., pp. 637–40.

73. Ibid., pp. 638–41.

74. Ibid., pp. 504, 641.

75. Turnbull, *The Theatre,* p. 77.

76. Talmadge, *Sports,* p. 232.

77. Mary C. Henderson, *The City and the Theatre* (Clifton, N.J., 1973), pp. 104–8.

78. Ibid., p. 108.

79. Turnbull, *The Theatre,* pp. 37–39.

80. Jeremiah Jeter, *A Discourse on the Immoral Tendencies of Theatrical Amusements* (Richmond, 1838), p. 10.

81. James Monroe Buckley, *Christians and the Theatre* (New York, 1875), p. 74.

82. Ibid., p. 75.

83. Ibid., p. 76.

84. Ibid., p. 75.

85. Turnbull, *The Theatre,* p. 197.

86. Herrick Johnson, *Plain Talk,* p. 34.

87. "A Letter to Respectable Ladies," pp. 415, 416.

88. Francis Wayland, *The Elements of Moral Science* (1835; reprint, Boston, 1846), p. 309.

89. Quoted by Samuel G. Winchester in *The Theatre* (New York, 1840), p. 199.

90. Winchester, *The Theatre,* p. 365.

91. Turnbull, *The Theatre,* p. 71.

92. Hill, *Theatrical Amusements,* p. 22.

93. Howe, "Victorian Culture," pp. 17–25; L. P. Brockett, *Woman: Her Rights, Privileges and Responsibilities* (1869; reprint, 1970), pp. 124–31.

94. Howe, "Victorian Culture," pp. 17–25; Rayne, *What Can a Woman Do?* pp. 447–81; Catherine Beecher and Harriet Beecher Stowe, *The American Woman's Home* (New York, 1869), passim; Brockett, *Woman*, pp. 124–31.

95. Rayne, *What Can a Woman Do?* p. 481; L. P. Brockett, *Woman: Her Rights, Privileges, and Responsibilities* (1869; reprint: 1970), pp. 124–31; Beecher, *Lectures*, passim.

96. Harvey Newcomb, *A Practical Directory for Young Christian Females* (1832; reprint: Boston, 1850), pp. 85, 86.

97. Washington Irving, "Letter IV" printed in *The Morning Chronicle*, 4 December 1802, in *The Complete Works of Washington Irving*, edited by B. T. Granger (Boston, 1977), pp. 12–18.

98. Charles Hayes Haswell, *Reminiscences of an Octogenarian of the City of New York, 1816–1860* (New York, 1896), p. 363.

99. Trollope, *Domestic Manners*, pp. 208, 209, 133, 243.

100. Stanley Hoole, *The Ante-Bellum Charleston Theatre* (Tuscaloosa, Ala., 1946), p. 14.

101. Maria Child, *Letters from New York*, 2d series (New York, 1845), p. 175.

102. Wood, *Personal Recollections*, pp. 143–47.

103. T. Allston Brown, *A History of the New York Stage: From the First Performance in 1732 to 1901*, vol. 1 (New York, 1903), p. 29.

104. Hone, *Diary*, p. 39.

105. Ibid., p. 109.

106. Brown, *History of the New York Stage*, vol. 1, p. 44.

107. Ibid., p. 123.

108. Richard Moody, *The Astor Place Riot* (Bloomington, Ind., 1958), passim.

109. Constance Rourke, *Troupers of the Gold Coast* (New York, 1928), p. 98.

110. Melvin H. Schoberlin, *From Footlights to Candles* (Denver, 1941), p. 18.

111. Skinner, *One Man*, p. 17.

112. Buckley, *Christians and the Theatre*, p. 63.

113. Turnbull, *The Theatre*, p. 99.

114. Buckley, *Christians and the Theatre*, p. 63.

115. Winchester, *The Theatre*, p. 196.

116. Brockett, *Woman*, p. 124.

117. Margaret Fuller Ossoli, *Woman in the Nineteenth Century* (Boston, 1855), p. 34.

118. Harriet Martineau, *Society in America*, vol. 2, (New York, 1962), p. 201; de Tocqueville, *Democracy*, vol. 2, pp. 213, 214.

119. Brockett, *Woman*, p. 89.

120. Rayne, *What Can a Woman Do?* p. 482.

121. Smith, *Theatrical Management*, p. 91; Mary Boykin Chestnut, *Diary from Dixie*, ed. Ben Ames Williams (Boston, 1949), p. 86.

122. Elizabeth Dexter, *Career Women of America, 1776–1840* (Francetown, New Hampshire, 1950), p. 224.

123. Fuller Ossoli, *Woman*, p. 218.

124. Brockett, *Woman*, p. 127.

125. Furnas, *The Americans*, p. 486.

126. Brockett, *Woman*, p. 127; Smith, *Theatrical Management*, p. 175.

127. Trollope, *Domestic Manners*, p. 275.

128. Ibid., p. 74.

129. J. S. Buckingham, *The Eastern and Western States of America in Three Volumes* (London, 1842), vol. 2, p. 395.

130. Trollope, *Domestic Manners*, p. 75.

131. Fuller Ossoli, *Woman*, p. 262; see also Winchester, *The Theatre*, p. 203.

132. Trollope, *Domestic Manners,* pp. 155, 156.

133. Eric Wollencott Barnes, *Lady of Fashion* (New York, 1954), p. 84.

134. Beth B. Gilchrist, *The Life of Mary Lyon* (Boston, 1910), p. 231.

135. Logan, *Before the Footlights,* p. 492.

136. Matilda Gage, *Women, Church and State* (1893; reprint: New York, 1972), p. 476.

137. Buckley, *Christians and the Theatre,* pp. 64, 65.

138. Ibid., p. 65.

139. David Hayes Agnew, *Theatrical Amusements* (Philadelphia, 1857), pp. 6, 7.

140. Olive Logan, *Apropos of Women and the Theatre* (New York, 1869), p. 8.

141. John Harold Wilson, *All the King's Ladies* (Chicago, 1958), p. 21.

142. Wilson, *All the King's Ladies,* pp. 14, 19–25, 71, 72.

143. Buckley, *Christians and the Theatre,* p. 126.

144. Turnbull, *The Theatre,* p. 92.

145. W. W. Clapp, *Record of the Boston Stage* (Boston, 1853), p. 298.

146. William Davidge, *The Drama Defended* (New York, 1859), pp. 13, 14.

147. Ibid., p. 36.

148. Ibid.

149. Mowatt, *Autobiography,* pp. 214–313.

150. Morris, *Life on the Stage,* p. 41.

151. Morris, *Stage Confidences,* pp. 192–96.

152. Joseph N. Ireland, *Mrs. Duff* (Boston, 1882), pp. 134–41.

153. Margaret Armstrong, *Fanny Kemble: Passionate Victorian* (New York, 1938), pp. 151, 153, 184; Fanny Kemble Wister, ed., *Fanny, The American Kemble: Her Journals and Unpublished Letters* (Tallahassee, Fla., 1972), pp. 37, 92.

154. Eric Wollencott Barnes, *Anna Cora: The Life and Theatre of Anna Cora Mowatt* (London, 1954), pp. 30, 76, 93, 94; Mowatt, *Autobiography,* pp, 37, 38, 142.

155. Theodore Roscoe, *The Web of Conspiracy* (New Jersey, 1959), p. 132.

## Chapter 2.  Enter the Breadwinner

1. Elizabeth Dexter, *Career Women of America: 1776–1840* (Francestown, N. H., 1950), p. 35.

2. Daniel Boorstin, *The Americans* (New York, 1958), p. 17.

3. Page Smith, *Daughters of the Promised Land* (Boston, 1970), pp. 37–76; Dexter, *Career Women,* p. 224.

4. A history of the broad economic developments in the nineteenth-century, reviewed on these pages, can be found in Boorstin, *The Americans,* Dexter, *Career Women,* and Barbara Wertheimer, *We Were There* (New York, 1977).

5. See Boorstin, *The Americans,* and Wertheimer, *We Were There.*

6. Mari Jo Buhle, Ann D. Gordon, and Nancy E. Schrom, *Women in American Society: A Historical Contribution* (Andover, Mass., 1973), p. 27.

7. Eliza Farrar, *The Young Lady's Friend* (1836; reprint: New York, 1974), p. 33.

8. Margaret Fuller Ossoli, *Women in the Nineteenth Century* (Boston, 1855), p. 218.

9. L. P. Brockett, *Woman: Her Rights, Privileges, and Responsibilities* (1869; reprint: New York, 1970), pp. 86–87. For an enlargement of the argument on religious grounds of women's subservience to man, see Matilda Gage, *Woman, Church and State* (1893; reprint: New York, 1972).

10. Brockett, *Woman,* pp. 89–97.

11. Ibid., p. 90.

12. Alexander Walker, *Woman Psychologically Considered as to Mind, Morals, Marriage, Matrimonial Slavery, Infidelity, Divorce* (New York, 1842), pp. 6, 7.

13. Dexter, *Career Women,* p. 224.

14. Buhle, Gordon and Schrom, *Women in American Society,* p. 27.

15. Ibid.

16. Fuller Ossoli, *Women in the Nineteenth Century,* p. 218.

17. Robert J. Moorehead, *Fighting the Devil's Triple Demons* (Philadelphia, 1911), p. 275.

18. Brocket, *Woman,* pp. 129, 130.

19. Wertheimer, *We Were There,* p. 61.

20. Ibid., pp. 61–84.

21. Ibid., p. 65.

22. Ibid., p. 95.

23. Ibid., p. 157.

24. Helen Campbell, *Women Wage Earners* (Boston, 1893), pp. 216–22.

25. Joseph A. Hill, *Women in Gainful Occupations, 1870 to 1920* (Washington, 1929), p. 42.

26. "Women's Work and Wages," *Harper's Magazine,* December, 1868, p. 666.

27. Brockett, *Woman,.* p. 130.

28. For the state of the American theater in the nineteenth century, reviewed in this chapter, see Bernard Hewitt, *Theatre U.S.A.* (New York, 1959); Richard Moody, *America Takes the Stage: Romanticism in American Drama and Theatre* (Bloomington, Ind., 1969); William Dunlap, *History of the American Theater* (1833; reprint: Philadelphia 1963); Noah Ludlow, *Dramatic Life as I Found It* (St. Louis, 1880), p. 347; and Alfred Bernheim, *The Business of the Theater* (New York, 1932).

29. Ludlow, *Dramatic Life,* passim.

30. Constance Rourke, *Troupers of the Gold Coast or the Rise of Lotta Crabtree* (New York, 1928), pp. 95, 96.

31. Ibid., p. 16.

32. James Gallegly, *Footlights on the Border* (The Hague, 1962), pp. 15, 47.

33. Moody, *America Takes the Stage,* p. 170.

34. Joseph Jefferson, *The Autobiography of Joseph Jefferson* (New York, 1889), p. 25.

35. Ludlow, *Dramatic Life,* p. 303.

36. Rourke, *Troupers,* p. 91.

37. William Mammen, *The Old Stock Company Style of Acting* (Boston, 1954), p. 10.

38. George C. D. Odell, *Annals of the New York Stage* (New York, 1927–49), vol. 6.

39. Jack Poggi, *Theater in America: The Impact of Economic Forces* (Ithaca, N.Y., 1968), pp. 3–22.

40. Dunlap, *History of the American Theater,* p. 331.

41. Ibid., p. 241.

42. John Bernard, *Retrospections on America, 1797–1811* (New York, 1887), pp. 259–63.

43. Mammen, *Old Stock Company Style,* p. 19.

44. Ibid., p. 19; Ludlow, *Dramatic Life,* pp. 470, 619, 715.

45. Dexter, *Career Women,* p. 89.

46. Hill, *Women in Gainful Occupations,* p. 42.

47. Mammen, *Old Stock Company Style,* p. 20.

48. William B. Wood., *Personal Recollections of the Stage* (Philadelphia, 1855), p. 406.

49. J. J. Jennings, *Theatrical and Circus Life* (St. Louis, 1882), pp. 245–47.

50. Clara Morris, *Life on the Stage; My Personal Experiences and Recollections,* (New York, 1901), pp. 58–60.

51. William Halliburton, *Effects of the Stage* (Boston, 1792), p. 71.

52. Clara Morris, *Stage Confidences,* (Boston, 1902), pp. 134, 135.

53. Olive Logan, *Before the Footlights and Behind the Scenes* (Philadelphia, 1870), p. 173.

54. Ibid., pp. 152, 153.

55. Morris, *Stage Confidences,* pp. 136, 137.

56. Morris, *Life on the Stage,* p. 20.

57. Matthew Carey, *Miscellaneous Pamphlets,* no. 12, cited in Helen L. Sumner's *History of Women in Industry* (Washington, 1910), pp. 127, 128.

58. Wertheimer, *We Were There,* p. 60.

59. Ibid.

60. William Sanger, *The History of Prostitution: Its Extent, Causes and Effects throughout the World* (New York, 1859), pp. 452–73, 527–29.

61. "A Working Woman's Statement," *The Nation,* 21 February 1867, p. 155.

62. "Women's Work and Wages," *Harper's Magazine,* December 1868, p. 667.

63. Gage, *Woman, Church and State,* pp. 459–60.

64. Horace Mann, "Eleventh Annual Report as Secretary of the State Board of Education of Massachusetts, 1847," *Cyclopedia of Education,* vol. 5, ed. Paul Monroe (New York, 1926), p. 509.

65. "Working Woman's Statement," p. 155.

66. Odell regularly cited the salaries of actresses and actors throughout his study of the New York stage. For additional information on the salaries and working conditions of ballet girls from the 1850s to 1900, see Logan, *Before the Footlights,* pp. 93–97; Jennings, *Theatrical and Circus Life,* pp. 245–47; and Davidge, *The Drama Defended* (New York, 1859), pp. 175–266.

67. Mammen, *Old Stock Company Style,* p. 38.

68. Jennings, *Theatrical and Circus Life,* pp. 241–47.

69. Dunlap, *History of the American Theatre,* pp. 70, 120.

70. Ibid., p. 148.

71. Wood, *Personal Recollections,* pp. 187, 200.

72. Logan, *Before the Footlights,* p. 445.

73. Mammen, *Old Stock Company Style,* p. 25.

74. George R. MacMinn, *Theatre of the Golden Era in California* (Caldwell, Idaho, 1941), p. 31.

75. Ibid., p. 31.

76. Ludlow, *Dramatic Life,* p. 451.

77. Morris, *Life on the Stage,* pp. 123–25.

78. Davidge, *Drama Defended,* p. 185.

79. Horace Mann, "Eleventh Annual Report," p. 509.

80. "Working Woman's Statement," p. 156.

81. "Women's Work and Wages," *Harper's Magazine,* p. 665.

82. Charles Elliott, "Women's Work and Wages," *North American Review,* August, 1882, pp. 146–49.

83. Gage, *Woman, Church and State,* p. 442.

84. Ibid.

85. Vera Brittain, *Lady into Woman: A History of Women from Victoria to Elizabeth II* (New York, 1953), p. 97.

86. Dexter, *Career Women,* p. 89.

87. Olive Logan, *Apropos of Women and the Theatre* (New York, 1869), pp. 15–17.

88. Dunlap, *History of the American Theater*, p. 120.

89. Ibid., p. 148.

90. Mowatt, *Autobiography*, pp. 330–31.

91. Henry Austin Clapp, *Reminiscences of a Dramatic Critic* (Boston, 1902), pp. 52, 232.

92. T. Allston Brown, *A History of the New York Stage: From the First Performance in 1732 to 1901*, vol. 1 (New York, 1903), p. 112.

93. Morris, *Life on the Stage*, p. 152.

94. Hewitt, pp. 133, 134.

95. Ludlow, p. 463.

96. George Vandenhoff, *Leaves from an Actor's Note-Book* (New York, 1860), p. 463.

97. Wood, *Personal Recollections*, p. 70.

98. Hewitt, *Theatre U.S.A.*, pp. 133, 134.

99. A simple check of Odell, *Annals,* and Brown, *History of the New York Stage,* yields many cast lists that include examples of common breeches roles.

100. Odell, *Annals,* passim, and Brown, *History of the New York Stage,* passim.

101. Mrs. John Drew, *Autobiographical Sketch of Mrs. John Drew* (New York, 1899), passim.

102. Bernard Falk, *The Naked Lady, or Storm over Adah* (London, 1934), passim.

103. Odell, *Annals,* vol. 7, p. 580.

104. Henry Austin Clapp, *Reminiscences of a Drama Critic* (Boston and New York, 1902), p. 220.

105. James Willis Yeater, *Charlotte Cushman, American Actress* (Urbana, Ill., 1959). passim.

106. MacMinn, *Theatre of the Golden Era*, p. 137.

107. Jefferson, *Autobiography*, pp. 154, 155.

108. Joe Cowell, *Thirty Years Passed among the Players* (New York, 1844), p. 101.

109. For information on Sarah Kirby-Stark, see MacMinn, *Theatre of the Golden Era,* pp. 70–80; and Rourke, *Troupers,* pp. 35–37.

110. MacMinn, *Theatre of the Golden Era,* p. 82.

111. For information on Catherine Sinclair, see MacMinn, *Theatre of the Golden Era,* pp. 138–46.; and Rourke, *Troupers,* pp. 77–80.

112. MacMinn, *Theatre of the Golden Era,* p. 141.

113. For information on Laura Keene, see MacMinn, *Theatre of the Golden Era,* pp. 91–94; and Odell, *Annals,* vol. 6, pp. 450–550, and vol. 7, pp. 126–309.

114. DeWitt Bodeen, *Ladies of the Footlights* (New York, 1937), p. 67.

115. Odell, *Annals,* vol. 6, p. 540.

116. Ibid., vol. 7, p. 255.

117. Ibid., p. 30.

118. Ibid., p. 474.

119. For information on Mrs. Drew, see her *Autobiographical Sketch.*

120. Moncure D. Conway, *The Theatre* (Cincinnati, 1857), pp. 21, 22.

121. Mowatt, *Autobiography,* p. 426.

122. Logan, *Before the Footlights,* p. 132.

123. Morris, *Stage Confidences,* p. 133.

124. Logan, *Before the Footlights,* p. 286.

## *Chapter 3.    Mary Ann Duff*

The chief source of information on the life of Mary Ann Duff is Joseph N. Ireland's biography. Briefer sketches and comments on Mrs. Duff appear in works by the following writers: Noah Ludlow, James E. Murdock, George C. D. Odell, H. P. Phelps, William Winter, and W. B. Wood.

1. William B. Wood, *Personal Recollections of the Stage* (Philadelphia, 1855), p. 406.

2. Joseph N. Ireland, *Mrs. Duff* (Boston, 1882), p. 28.

3. "Mrs. Duff," *Boston Gazette,* March 1821.

4. George C. D. Odell, *Annals of the American Stage* (1927–49), vol. 4, p. 90.

5. "Mrs. Duff's Benefit," *Boston Commercial Gazette,* 4 October 1824, p. 2.

6. Ireland, *Mrs. Duff,* p. 45.

7. "The Drama," *New York Albion,* 10 February 1827, p. 280.

8. "Mrs. Duff," *New York Mirror,* 5 May 1827, p. 327.

9. Ireland, *Mrs. Duff,* pp. 97, 98.

10. James E. Murdock, *The Stage, of Recollections of Actors and Acting from an Experience of Fifty Years* (Philadelphia, 1880), p. 267.

11. Ireland, *Mrs. Duff,* p. 121.

12. Ibid.

13. Ibid., p. 120.

14. Ibid., pp. 122, 123.

15. Ibid., p. 134.

16. William Winter, *Wallet of Time* (New York, 1913), p. 65.

17. Ibid., pp. 66, 67.

18. Noah Ludlow, *Dramatic Life as I Found It* (St. Louis, 1880), p. 467.

19. Manuscripts held by Boston Public Library.

## Chapter 4.    Fanny Kemble

The primary sources of information on Fanny Kemble are her journals, listed in the bibliography under her name. Many biographies of her have been written, including works by Margaret Armstrong, Mrs. Dorothie Bobbe, Henrietta Buckmaster, Leota Driver, Henry Gibbs, Dorothy Marshall, and Robert Rushmore. Estimates of Fanny Kemble can also be found in many of the standard histories of the theater.

1. Fanny Kemble Wister, ed., *Fanny, The American Kemble: Her Journals and Unpublished Letters* (Tallahassee, Fla., 1972), p. 34.

2. Margaret Armstrong, *Fanny Kemble: A Passionate Victorian* (New York, 1938), p. 81.

3. Wister, *Fanny,* p. 5.

4. Armstrong, *Fanny Kemble,* p. 14.

5. Ibid., p. 82.

6. Wister, *Fanny,* p. 42.

7. Ibid., p. 37.

8. William B. Wood, *Personal Recollections of the Stage* (Philadelphia, 1855), p. 368.

9. Philip Hone, *The Diary of Philip Hone, 1828–1851,* ed. Allan Nevins (New York, 1936), p. 573.

10. Walt Whitman, "Walt Whitman on Fanny Kemble," *New York Dramatic Mirror,* 17 May 1879, p. 6.

11. Armstrong, *Fanny Kemble,* p. 165.

12. Wister, *Fanny,* p. 134.

13. Fanny Kemble, *Further Records* (New York, 1891), p. 359.

14. Herman Melville, "Letter to Evert Duyckinck," 2 February 1899, *Letters of Herman Melville*, ed. Merrill D. Davis and William H. Gilman (New Haven, 1960), pp. 77, 78.

15. Joseph Adams Smith, *Taghconic* (Boston, 1852), p. 107.

16. Kemble, *Further Records*, p. 190.

17. Wister, *Fanny*, p. 2.

18. Armstrong, *Fanny Kemble*, p. 325.

## Chapter 5.    Charlotte Cushman

There is at least some mention of Charlotte Cushman in every theatrical history of her day. Biographies devoted to Cushman have been written by Lawrence Barrett, Clara Clement, Joseph Leach, William Price, Emma Stebbins, Mrs. D. Walker, and James Willis Yeater.

1. James Murdock, *The Stage, or Recollections of Actors and Acting from an Experience of Fifty Years* (Philadelphia, 1880), p. 239.

2. Clara Clement, *Charlotte Cushman* (Boston, 1882), pp. 10, 11.

3. Ibid.

4. John Coleman, *Fifty Years of an Actor's Life* (New York, 1904), vol, 3., pp. 362–63.

5. Emma Stebbins, *Charlotte Cushman* (Boston, 1878), p. 17.

6. Ibid.

7. Willian Winter, *Other Days* (New York, 1908), p. 154.

8. Westland Marsden, *Our Recent Actors* (London, 1888), pp. 147, 75, 76.

9. Coleman, *Fifty Years*, p. 363.

10. George C. D. Odell, *Annals of the American Stage* (New York, 1927–49), vol, 4, p. 147.

11. Stebbins, *Charlotte Cushman*, p. 170.

## Chapter 6.    Anna Cora Mowatt

The best sources of information on Anna Cora Mowatt remain her own *Autobiography of an Actress* and splendid biographies by Eric Barnes and Marius Blesi.

1. Anna Cora Mowatt, *Autobiography of an Actress* (Boston, 1854), p. 38.

2. Ibid., p. 137.

3. Ibid., p. 138.

4. Eric Wollencott Barnes, *The Lady of Fashion* (New York, 1954), p. 76.

5. Ibid., p. 84.

6. Eric Wollencott Barnes, *Anna Cora: The Life and Theatre of Anna Cora Mowatt* (London, 1954), p. 150.

7. Laurence Hutton, *Curiosities of the American Stage* (New York: Harper and Brothers, 1891), p. 67.

8. Mowatt, *Autobiography*, p. 347:

## Chapter 7.    Laura Keene

The following sources on the life of Laura Keene are not always accurate and not complete, but they are all that we have on her early life: the Creahan and Donahoe biographies and the two articles in the *Dramatic Mirror*. Information on her involvement in investigations following Lincoln's death can be found in Theodore Roscoe's book on the assassination, *The Web of Conspiracy,* and in studies of the life of Edwin Booth. Books on the California theater contain information about her experiences in the West, and the memoirs of actors who worked with her have brief sketches of her character and career.

1. John Creahan, *The Life of Laura Keene* (Philadelphia, 1897), p. 167.
2. Ibid.
3. Kate Reignolds-Winslow, *Yesterday with Actors* (Boston, 1887), pp. 71, 72.
4. Creahan, *Life of Laura Keene,* pp. 135, 136.
5. William Winter, *Vagrant Memories* (New York, 1915), pp. 46–58.
6. Seaton Munroe, "Recollections of Lincoln's Assassination," *North American Review,* no. 473, April 1896, p. 425.

## Chapter 8.    Adah Isaacs Menken

Books on Adah Isaacs Menken include her own book of poems, *Infelicia,* and books by George L. Barclay, James Edwin, Bernard Falk, Nathaniel Fleischer, Noel Bertram Gerson, Allan Lesser, and Richard Northcott.

The controversy and uncertainty about the life of Adah Menken have affected current criticism of her life. Much new material about her appears in a biography, *Queen of the Plaza,* written by Noel Gerson. He based his study on an unpublished diary kept by Adah and an autobiographical fragment. The fragment was widely published and is readily available; the diary is, however, another story. Unfortunately, Mr. Gerson's bibliographical note that the diary is held by Harvard University appears to be incorrect. Neither the diary nor the collection cited by Gerson is, according to Harvard librarians, in any of their collections. Private correspondence with Mr. Gerson has failed to jog his memory about where he did use the diary. Harvard has not been able to locate it; it is not listed in catalogs of manuscript collections; and extensive correspondence with other collections has failed to reveal the location of the diary as of this writing. Until that document is located, the information about Adah taken from the diary has to be considered unsubstantiated: that she was a prostitute in Havana, that she continued to be promiscuous for most of her life, that she did not appear onstage until after her marriage to Menken, and other details from the Gerson book. Information that appears in the Gerson book alone is identified in the text.

1. Allan Lesser, *Enchanting Rebel: The Secret of Adah Isaacs Menken* (Philadelphia, 1947), p. 22.
2. James Murdock, *The Stage, of Recollections of Actors and Acting from an Experience of Fifty Years* (Philadelphia, 1880), pp. 286–89.
3. Lesser, *Enchanting Rebel,* p. 49.
4. Ibid., p. 53.

5. Henry P. Phelps, *Players of a Century: A Record of the Albany Stage* (Albany, N.Y., 1880), p. 310.

6. Constance Rourke, *Troupers of the Gold Coast or the Rise of Lotta Crabtree* (New York, 1928), p. 176.

7. Phelps, *Players of a Century,* pp. 315, 316.

## *Chapter 9.   Lotta Crabtree*

The most useful biography of Charlotte "Lotta" Crabtree's California years is Constance Rourke's *Troupers of the Gold Coast.* Her later career on tour in the East is the subject of a firsthand account by an actress who worked with her, Helen Marie Bates. Another study of Lotta's life which includes detailed information on her retirement years and the controversy over her will is by David K. Dempsey. Other useful information is contained in MacMinn's and Gagey's histories of the California stage.

1. Constance Rourke, *Troupers of the Gold Coast or the Rise of Lotta Crabtree* (New York, 1928), p. 81.

2. David K. Dempsey, *The Triumphs and Trials of Lotta Crabtree* (New York, 1968), p. 113.

3. Rourke, *Troupers of the Gold Coast,* p. 107.

4. "Amusements," *New York Times,* 30 July 1867, p. 5.

5. Helen Marie Bates, *Lotta's Last Season* (Brattleboro, Vt., 1940), p. 15.

6. Ibid., p. 42.

7. Ibid., p. 15.

8. Ibid., p. 31.

9. Dempsey, *Triumphs and Trials,* p. 158.

10. Rourke, *Troupers,* pp. 203, 205.

11. Ibid., p. 205.

# BIBLIOGRAPHY

Agnew, David Hayes. *Theatrical Amusements*. Philadelphia: W. S. Young, 1857.

Ahlstrom, Sidney. *The Religious History of the American People*. New Haven: Yale University Press, 1972.

"Amusements," *New York Times,* 30 July 1867, p. 5.

Armstrong, Margaret. *Fanny Kemble: A Passionate Victorian*. New York: Macmillan, 1938.

Barclay, George Leppard. *The Life and Remarkable Career of Adah Isaacs Menken*. Philadelphia: Barclay and Co., 1868.

Barnes, Eric Wollencott, *Anna Cora: The Life and Theatre of Anna Cora Mowatt*. London: Secker and Warbury, 1954.

Barnes, Eric Wollencott. *The Lady of Fashion*. New York: Charles Scribners' Sons, 1954.

Barrett, Lawrence. *Charlotte Cushman*. New York: Burt Franklin, 1889.

Bates, Helen Marie. *Lotta's Last Season*. Brattleboro, Vt.: E. L. Hildreth and Co., 1940.

Beecher, Catherine, and Harriet Beecher Stowe. *The American Woman's Home*. 1869; reprint: New York: Arno Press, 1971.

Beecher, Henry Ward. *Lectures to Young Men*. New York: J. P. Jewett, 1856.

Bennett, Helen Marie. *Women and Work*. New York: D. Appleton and Co., 1917.

Bernheim, Alfred. *The Business of the Theatre*. New York: Benjamin Blom, 1932.

Blesi, Marius. *The Life and Letters of Anna Cora Mowatt*. Charlottesville: University of Virginia Press, 1952.

Boardman, James. *America and the Americans by a Citizen of the World*. London: Longman and Rees, 1833.

Bobbe, Mrs. Dorothie. *Fanny Kemble*. New York: Minton, Balch and Co., 1931.

Bode, Carl, ed. *Midcentury America*. Carbondale: Southern Illinois University Press, 1972.

Bodeen, DeWitt. *Ladies of the Footlights*. New York: Login Press, 1937.

Bodichon, Barbara. *Women and Work*. New York: C. S. Francis and Co., 1859.

Boorstin, Daniel. *The Americans*. 3 vols. New York: Vintage Press, 1974.

Brittain, Vera, *Lady into Woman*. New York: Macmillan, 1953.

Brockett, L. P. *Woman: Her Rights, Privileges and Responsibilities*. 1869; reprint: Freeport, N.Y.: Books for Libraries Press, 1970.

Brown, T. Allston. *A History of the New York Stage: From the First Performance in 1732 to 1901*. 3 vols. New York: Dodd, Mead and Co., 1903.

Buckingham, J. S. *The Eastern and Western States of America in Three Volumes*. London: Fisher, Son and Co., 1842.

Buckley, James Monroe. *Christians and the Theatre*. New York: Nelson and Phillips, 1875.

Buckmaster, Henrietta. *Fire in the Heart*. New York: Harcourt Brace, 1948.

Buhle, Mari Jo, Ann D. Gordon, and Nancy E. Schrom. *Women in American Society*. Andover, Mass.: Manuscript Modular Pubns., 1973.

Campbell, Helen. *Women Wage Earners*. Boston: Roberts Bros., 1893.

Carey, Matthew. *Miscellaneous Pamphlets*, no. 12. Included in Helen L. Sumner's *History of Women in Industry*. Washington, D.C.: U.S. Government Printing Office, 1910, pp. 127–28.

Chestnut, Mary Boykin. *Diary from Dixie*, edited by Ben Ames Williams. Boston: Houghton Mifflin Co., 1949.

Child, Maria. *Letters from New York*. 2d series. New York: C. S. Francis and Co., 1845.

Clapp, Henry Austin. *Reminiscences of a Dramatic Critic*. Boston and New York: Houghton Mifflin, 1902.

Clapp, W. W. *Record of the Boston Stage*. Boston: J. Monroe, 1853.

Clement, Clara Erskine. *Charlotte Cushman*. Boston: James R. Osgood and Co., 1882.

Coleman, John. *Fifty Years of an Actor's Life*. 2 vols. New York: James Pott and Co., 1904.

"Confessions of an Actress" *New York Morning Herald*, 19 September 1838, p. 1.

Conklin, Mabel. *How Women May Earn a Living*. New York: C. Francis, Printers, 1907.

Conway, Monroe D. *The Theatre*. Cincinnati: Truman and Spofford, 1857.

Cowell, Joe. *Thirty Years Passed among the Players in England and America*. New York: Harper and Bros., 1844.

Crawford, Mary Caroline. *Romance of the American Theatre*. Boston: Little, Brown, 1924.

Creahan, John. *The Life of Laura Keene*. Philadelphia: Rodgers Pub. Co., 1897.

Davidge, William. *The Drama Defended*. New York: Samuel French, 1859.

Davidge, William. *Footlight Flashes*. New York: American News Co., 1866.

Dempsey, David K. *The Triumphs and Trials of Lotta Crabtree*. New York: Marros, 1968.

Dexter, Elizabeth. *Career Women of America: 1776–1840*. Francestown, N.H.: Marshall Jones and Co. 1950.

Dickens, Charles. *American Notes*. 2 vols. London: Chapman and Hall, 1842.

Dimmick, Ruth Crosby. *Our Theatres Today*. New York: H.K. Fly, 1913.

Donahoe, Joseph Aloysius. *Laura Keene*. Wilmington, Del.: n.p., 1928.

Douglass, Ann. *The Feminization of American Culture*. New York: Knopf, 1977.

"The Drama." *New York Albion*, 10 February 1827, p. 280.

Drew, Mrs. John. *Autobiographical Sketch of Mrs. John Drew*. New York: Charles Scribner's Sons, 1899.

Driver, Leota Stultz. *Fanny Kemble*. New York: Negro University Press, 1969.

Duer, William Alexander. *Reminiscences of an Old New Yorker*. New York: W. L. Andrews, 1867.

Dunlap, William. *Diary of William Dunlap (1766–1839)*. New York: New York Historical Society, 1930.

Dunlap, William. *History of the American Theatre*. New York: Burt Franklin, 1963.

Dwight, Timothy. *An Essay on the Stage*. Middletown, Conn.: Sharp, Jones and Co., 1824.

Edwin, James. *Biography of Adah Isaacs Menken*. New York: E. James, 1881.

Elliott, Charles. "Women, Work and Wages." *North American Review*, August, 1882, pp. 146–51.

Everts, William W. *The Theatre*. Chicago: Church and Goodman, 1866.

Faithfull, Emily. *Three Visits to America*. New York: Fowler and Wells Co., 1884.

Falk, Bernard. *The Naked Lady or Storm over Adah*. London: Hutchinson and Co., 1934.

Farrar, Eliza. *The Young Lady's Friend.* 1836; reprint: New York: Arno Press, 1974.

Fleischer, Nathaniel S. *Reckless Lady.* New York: Press of C. J. O'Brien, 1941.

Ford, Tom, *A Peep behind the Curtain by a Supernumerary.* Boston: Redding and Co., 1850.

Frohman, Daniel. *Daniel Frohman Presents.* New York: C. Kendall and W. Sharp, 1935.

Furnas, J. C. *The Americans: A Social History of the United States.* New York: G. P. Putnam's Sons, 1969.

Gage, Matilda. *Women, Church and State.* 1893; reprint: New York: Arno Press, 1972.

Gagey, Edmond. *The San Francisco Stage.* New York: Columbia University Press, 1950.

Gallegly, James. *Footlights on the Border.* The Hague: Mouton. 1962.

Gerson, Noel Bertram. *Queen of the Plaza.* New York: Funk and Wagnalls, 1962.

Gibbs, Henry. *Affectionately Yours, Fanny.* London: Jarrolds, 1947.

Gilbert, Ann. *The Stage Reminiscences of Mrs. Gilbert.* Edited by Charlotte M. Martin. New York: Charles Scribner's Sons, 1901.

Gilchrist, Beth B. *The Life of Mary Lyon.* Boston: Houghton Mifflin, 1910.

Gilder, Rosamund. *Enter the Actress.* New York: Houghton Mifflin, 1931.

Gouley, George F. *The Legitimate Drama.* Washington, D.C: W. H. Moore, 1857.

Gow, Alexander M. *Good Morals and Gentle Manners for Schools and Families.* New York: American Book Co., 1873.

Grattan, Thomas Colley. *Civilized America.* 1859; reprint: New York: Johnson Reprint Corp., 1969.

Grimsted, David. *Melodrama Unveiled.* Chicago: University of Chicago Press, 1968.

Gurley, Phineas Densmore. *The Voice of the Rod.* Washington, D.C.: Ballantyne, 1865.

Halliburton, William. *Effects of the Stage.* Boston: Young and Etheridge, 1792.

Haswell, Charles Hayes. *Reminiscences of an Octogenarian of the City of New York (1816–1860).* New York: Harper and Bros., 1896.

Hatfield, Robert M. *The Theatre.* Chicago: Methodist Book Depository, 1866.

Henderson, Mary C. *The City and the Theatre.* Clifton, N.J.: James White Company, 1973.

Hewitt, Bernard. *Theatre U.S.A. 1668 to 1957.* New York: McGraw-Hill, 1959.

Hill, Joseph A. *Women in Gainful Occupations 1870–1920.* Washington, D.C.: U.S. Government Printing Office, 1929.

Hill, Stephen P. *Theatrical Amusements.* Philadelphia: Baptist General Tract Society, 1830.

Hodgkinson, John. *Narrative of His Connection with the Old America Company.* New York: J. Oram, 1797.

Hone, Philip. *The Diary of Philip Hone, 1828–1851,* Edited by Allan Nevins. New York: Dodd, Mead and Co., 1936

Hoole, Stanley, *The Ante Bellum Charleston Theatre.* Tuscaloosa: University of Alabama Press, 1946.

Hornblow, Arthur. *A History of the Theatre in America from Its Beginnings to the Present Time.* 2 vols. Philadelphia and London: J. B. Lippincott, 1919.

Howe, Daniel. "Victorian Culture in America." In *Victorian America.* Philadelphia: University of Pennsylvania Press, 1976.

Howison, John. *Sketches of Upper Canada.* Edinburgh: Oliver and Boyd, 1821.

Hudson, Winthrop. *American Protestantism.* Chicago: University of Chicago Press, 1961.

Hunt, Gaillard. *Life in America.* New York: Harper and Bros., 1914.

Hutchins, Grace. *Women Who Work.* New York: International Pub. 1934.

Hutton, Laurence. *Curiosities of the American Stage.* New York: Harper and Bros., 1891.

Ireland, Joseph N. *Mrs. Duff.* Boston: James R. Osgood and Co., 1882.

Ireland, Joseph N. *Records of the New York Stage from 1750 to 1860.* 2 vols. New York: T. H. Morrell, 1866–67.

Irving, Washington. "Letter IV" printed in *Morning Chronicle,* 4 December 1802. *In Complete Works of Washington Irving.* Boston: Twayne, 1977.

James, Reese Davis. *Old Drury of Philadelphia: A History of the Philadelphia Stage, 1800– 1835.* Philadelphia: Greenwood Press, 1930.

Jefferson, Joseph. *The Autobiography of Joseph Jefferson.* New York: New Century Co., 1889.

Jenkins, Stephen. *The Greatest Street in the World.* New York: G. P. Putnam's Sons, 1911.

Jennings, John J. *Theatrical and Circus Life: Or Secrets of the Stage, Green-Room and Sawdust Arena.* St. Louis: Sun Pub. Co., 1882.

Jeter, Jeremiah Bell. *A Discourse on the Immoral Tendency of Theatrical Amusements.* Richmond: W. MacFarland, 1838.

Johnson, Claudia D. "That Guilty Third Tier." In *Victorian America,* edited by Daniel Howe. Philadelphia: University of Pennsylvania Press, 1976.

Johnson, Herrick. *A Plain Talk about the Theatre.* Chicago: F. H. Revel, 1882.

Kemble, Fanny. *Journal from August 1, 1832 to July 17, 1833.* Philadelphia: Lea and Blanchard, 1835.

Kemble, Fanny. *Journal of a Residence in America.* Paris: n.p., 1835.

Kemble, Fanny. *Journal of a Residence on a Georgia Plantation.* New York: Harper and Bros., 1864.

Kemble, Fanny. *On the Stage.* New York: Dramatic Museum of Columbia University, 1926.

Kemble, Fanny. *Records of a Girlhood.* New York: H. Holt and Co., 1879.

Kemble, Fanny. *Records of Later Life.* New York: H. Holt and Co., 1882.

Kimmell, Stanley. *The Mad Booths of Maryland.* New York: Bobbs-Merrill, 1940.

Klinkowstrom, Baron. *America, 1818–1820.* Translated and edited by Franklin D. Scott. Evanston, Ill.: Northwestern University Press, 1952.

"Ladies of New York Look Well to This Thing," *New York Morning Herald,* 19 September 1838, p. 2.

Larkins, Oliver. *Art and Life in America.* New York: Holt, Rinehart, and Winston, 1960.

"Laura Keene's Early Career," *New York Daily Mirror,* 22 January 1887, p. 7.

Leach, Joseph. *Bright Particular Star.* New Haven: Yale University Press, 1970.

Leman, Walter. *Memories of an Old Actor.* San Francisco: A Roman Co., 1886.

Lerner, Gerda. *The Lady and the Mill Girl.* Andover, Mass.: Warner Modular Pubns., 1973.

Lesser, Allen. *Enchanting Rebel: The Secret of Adah Isaacs Menken.* Philadelphia: Ruttle, Shaw and Wetherill, 1947.

"A Letter to Respectable Ladies Who Frequent the Theatre." *The Christian Spectator.* Vol. I New series. August 1827; pp. 411, 412.

Lewis, George. *Impressions of America and the American Churches.* 1848; reprint: New York: Negro University Press, 1968.

Logan, Olive. *Apropos of Women and the Theatre.* New York: Carleton Pub., 1869.

Logan, Olive. *Before the Footlights and behind the Scenes.* Philadelphia: Parmelee and Co., 1870.

Ludlow, Noah M. *Dramatic Life as I Found It.* St. Louis: G. I. Jones and Co., 1880.

McGlinchee, Claire. *The First Decade of the Boston Museum.* Boston: Humphries, 1940.

McIntosh, Maria. *Woman in America: Her Work and Her Reward.* New York: D. Appleton and Co., 1850.

MacMinn, G. R. *Theatre of the Golden Era in California.* Caldwell, Idaho: Caxton Printers, 1941.

McVicker, J. H. *The Press, the Pulpit and the Stage.* Chicago: Western News Co., 1883.

Mann, Horace, "Eleventh Annual Report as Secretary of the State Board of Education in Massachusetts, 1847." *Cyclopedia of Education.* vol. 5. Edited by Paul Monroe. New York: Macmillan, 1926, p. 509.

Marryat, Frederick. *A Diary in America with Remarks on Its Institutions.* New York: Knopf, 1962.

Marston, John Westland. *Our Recent Actors.* London: S. Low, Marston, Searle, 1888.

Martineau, Harriet. *Society in America.* 2 vols. New York: Saunders and Otley, 1962.

Melville, Herman, *The Letters of Herman Melville.* Edited by Merrill D. Davis and William H. Gilman. New Haven: Yale University Press, 1960.

Menken, Adah Isaacs. *Infelicia.* New York: H. L. Williams, 1868.

Mesick, Jane Louise. *The English Traveller in America, 1785–1835.* New York: Columbia University Press, 1922.

Minniegerode, Mead. *The Fabulous Forties, 1840–1850.* New York: G. P. Putnam's Sons, 1924.

Moody, Richard. *America Takes the Stage.* Bloomington: Indiana University Press, 1955.

Moody, Richard. *The Astor Place Riot.* Bloomington: Indiana University Press, 1958.

Moody, Richard. *Dramas from the American Theatre, 1762–1909.* New York: World, 1966.

Moorehead, Robert J. *Fighting the Devil's Triple Demons.* Philadelphia: National Pub. Co., 1911.

Morris, Clara. *Life on the Stage.* New York: McClure, Phillips and Co., 1901.

Morris, Clara. *The Life of a Star.* New York: McClure, Phillips and Co., 1906.

Morris, Clara. *Stage Confidences.* Boston: Lothrop Pub. Co., 1902.

Morris, Lloyd. *Incredible New York.* New York: Random House, 1951.

Mott, Frank Luther. *Golden Multitudes.* New York: Macmillan, 1947.

Mowatt, Anna Cora. *Autobiography of An Actress.* Boston: Ticknor, Reed and Fields, 1854.

Mowatt, Anna Cora. *Mimic Life or before and behind the Curtain.* Boston: Ticknor, Reed and Fields, 1855.

"Mrs. Duff." *Boston Gazette,* March 1921.

"Mrs. Duff." *New York Mirror,* 5 May 1827, p. 327.

Munroe, Seaton. "Recollections of Lincoln's Assassination." *North American Review,* no. 473 (April 1896), p. 425.

Murdock, James. *The Stage, of Recollections of Actors and Acting from an Experience of Fifty Years.* Philadelphia: J. M. Stoddard and Co., 1880.

Murtagh, John M., and Sara Harris. *Cast the First Stone.* New York: McGraw-Hill, 1957.

Newcomb, Harvey. *A Practical Directory for Young Christian Females Being a Series of Letters from a Brother to a Sister.* Boston: Sabbath School Society, 1850.

Northcott, Richard. *Adah Isaacs Menken.* London: The Press Printers, 1921.

Odell, George C. D. *Annals of the New York Stage.* 15 vols. New York: Columbia University Press, 1927–1949.

Ossoli, Margaret Fuller. *Women in the Nineteenth Century.* 1847; reprint: New York: Greenwood Press, 1968.

Palmer, A. M. "American Theatres." In *One Hundred Years of American Commerce,* edited by Chauncy Depew. New York: D. O. Haynes and Co., 1895. Vol. 1, pp. 157–65.

Peltzer, Otto. *The Church and the Theatre.* Chicago: D. Fraser and Sons, 1882.

Peltzer, Otto. *The Moralist and the Theatre.* Chicago: D. Fraser and Sons, 1887.

Phelps, Henry P. *Players of a Century: A Record of the Albany Stage.* Albany: J. Mc-
Donough, 1880.

Philander. "To The Printer." *New York Gazette;* 24 December 1761, p. 3.

Philander. "To The Printer." *New York Journal;* 7 January 1768–11 February 1768,
p. 2.

Poggi, Jack. *Theatre in America: The Impact of Economic Forces.* Ithaca, N.Y.: Cornell
University Press, 1968.

Power, Tyrone. *Impressions of America during the Years 1833–1834.* London: Richard
Bentley, 1836.

Price, William Thompson. *A Life of Charlotte Cushman.* New York: Brentano Press,
1894.

Rayne, Martha. *What Can a Woman Do?* Nid.; reprint: New York: Arno Press, 1974.

Reignolds-Winslow, Catherine. *Yesterday with Actors.* Boston: Cupples and Hurd,
1887.

"The Romance of Laura Keene." *New York Dramatic Mirror;* 15 January 1887, p. 6.

Roscoe, Theodore. *The Web of Conspiracy.* Englewood Cliffs; N.J.: Prentice-Hall, 1959.

Rourke, Constance. *Troupers of the Gold Coast or the Rise of Lotta Crabtree.* New York:
Harcourt Brace and Co., 1928.

R. S. "To the Printer." *New York Journal,* 28 January 1768. p. 2.

Ruggles, Eleanor. *Prince of Players: Edwin Booth.* New York: W. W. Norton Co.,
1953.

Rushmore, Robert. *Fanny Kemble.* New York: Crowell-Collier Press, 1970.

Ryan, Kate. *Old Boston Museum Days.* Boston: Little, Brown, 1915.

Sanger, William W. *A History of Prostitution.* New York: Harper and Bros., 1858.

Schoberlin, Melvin H. *From Candles to Footlights.* Denver: Old West Pub. Co., 1941.

Simcox, Edith. "The Industrial Employment of Women." *Frazer's Magazine,* February
1897, p. 246.

Skinner, Maud. *One Man in His Time: The Adventures of H. Watkins, Strolling Player,
1846–1863.* Philadelphia: University of Pennsylvania Press, 1938.

Sklar, Catherine K. *Catherine Beecher. A Study in American Domesticity.* New Haven:
Yale University Press, 1973.

Smith, Joseph Adams. *Taghconic.* Boston: n.p., 1852.

Smith, Page. *Daughters of the Promised Land.* Boston: Little, Brown, 1970.

Smith, Sol. *Theatrical Management in the South and West.* New York: Benjamin Blom,
1868.

Sonneck, O. G. *Early Concert Life in America.* New York: Musurgia, 1949.

Stebbins, Emma. *Charlotte Cushman: Her Life, Letters, and Memories.* Boston: Houghton
Osgood and Co., 1878.

Talmadge, Thomas DeWitt. *Sports That Kill.* New York: Harper and Bros., 1875.

Taubman, Howard. *The Making of the American Theatre.* New York: Howard McCann,
1965.

"The Theatre." *New York Morning Herald.* 1 November 1842, p. 2.

Thompson, J. F. *A Discourse on the Character and Influence of the Theater,* New York,
n.p., 1847.

Tocqueville, Alexis de. *Democracy in America.* 1851; reprint: New York: Oxford University Press, 1951.

Towse, John Ranken. *Sixty Years of the Theatre.* New York: Funk and Wagnalls, 1916.

Trollope, Francis. *Domestic Manners of the Americans.* 1832; reprint: New York: Knopf,
1949.

Turnbull, Robert. *The Theatre.* Hartford: Caufield and Robins, 1837.

Turnbull, Robert. *The Theatre in Its Influence upon Literature, Morals and Religion.* Boston:
Gould, Kendall and Lincoln, 1839.

Vandenhoff, George. *Leaves from an Actor's Notebook*. New York: D. Appleton and Co., 1860.

Walker, Alexander. *Women Psychologically Considered*. New York: Holland, 1842.

Walker, Mrs. D. *Reminiscences of the Life of the World-Renowned Charlotte Cushman*. Boston: W. P. Tennay, 1876.

Ware, John T. *May I Go to the Theatre*. Baltimore: Sun Printing, 1871.

Waters, Clara. *Charlotte Cushman*. Boston: J. R. Osgood, 1882.

Wayland, Francis. *The Elements of Moral Science*. 1835; reprint: Boston: Gould, Kendall and Lincoln, 1846.

Wertheimer, Barbara. *We Were There*. New York: Pantheon Books, 1977.

Westermarc, Edward. *The Origin and Development of the Moral Ideas*. New York: Books for Libraries Press, 1906.

Whitman, Walt. "Walt Whitman on Fanny Kemble." *New York Dramatic Mirror*, 17 May 1879, p. 6.

Wilson, Garff B. *A History of American Acting*. Bloomington: Indiana University Press, 1966.

Wilson, John Harold. *All the King's Ladies*. Chicago: University of Chicago Press, 1958.

Winchester, Samuel G. *The Theatre*. New York: W. S. Martien, 1840.

Winter, William. *Life and Art of Joseph Jefferson*. New York: Moffat, Yard, and Co., 1901.

Winter, William. *Other Days*. New York: Moffat, Yard and Co., 1901.

Winter, William. *The Press and the Stage*. New York: Lockwood and Coombes, 1889.

Winter, William. *Vagrant Memories*. New York: George H. Doran and Co., 1915.

Winter, William. *Wallet of Time*. 2 vols. New York: Moffat, Yard and Co., 1913.

Wise, Winifred Esther. *Fanny Kemble*. New York: G. P. Putnam's Sons, 1967.

Wister, Fanny Kemble, ed. *Fanny: The American Kemble*. Tallahassee, Fla. South Pass Press, 1972.

"Women's Work and Wages."*Harper's Magazine*, December 1868, pp. 665–67.

Wood, William B. *Personal Recollections of the Stage*. Philadelphia: H. S. Baird, 1855.

"A Working Woman's Statement." *The Nation*, 2 February 1867, pp. 155–56.

Yeater, James Willis. *Charlotte Cushman, American Actress*. Urbana: University of Illinois Press, 1959.

# INDEX